Educational Planning of Court-Involved Youth

Educational Planning of Court-Involved Youth provides a framework for alleviating chronic barriers for youth in the child welfare and juvenile justice systems. This guide combines best-practice recommendations from national research with direct service tactics employed successfully in multiple counties. Included are the necessary components to implement a collaborative, community-centered intervention system that meets the needs of the county, family, and individual. With the understanding that each county carries its own strengths, barriers, and resources, these tools serve as a model for assessing and adapting the system to cater to the unique needs of each area in which it is implemented. This text helps facilitate the coordination and collaboration necessary to foster comprehensive systems and individualized planning for youth.

Amy M. Bishop, MSW, received her Master of Social Work from the University of Denver. She has worked in educational advocacy and consulting for over ten years. She works as an education consultant for families, youth, schools, and agencies in improving educational outcomes and conducts training and workshops nationwide on the educational needs of court-involved and at-risk youth.

Educational Planning of Court-Involved Youth

A Guide for Counties, Systems, and Individuals

Amy M. Bishop, MSW

Routledge
Taylor & Francis Group

NEW YORK AND LONDON

First published 2019
by Routledge
52 Vanderbilt Avenue, New York, NY 10017

and by Routledge
2 Park Square, Milton Park, Abingdon, Oxon, OX14 4RN

Routledge is an imprint of the Taylor & Francis Group, an informa business

© 2019 Taylor & Francis

Library of Congress Cataloging-in-Publication Data
A catalog record for this title has been requested

ISBN: 978-1-138-31383-5 (hbk)
ISBN: 978-1-138-31384-2 (pbk)
ISBN: 978-0-429-45740-1 (ebk)

Typeset in Gill Sans
by Deanta Global Publishing Services, Chennai, India

Visit the eResources: www.routledge.com/9781138313842

To all of the amazing youth with whom I have had the privilege of working in the last eleven years. You are truly my inspiration in believing change is possible. You overcome barriers every day to achieve your dreams, thank you for letting me be a part of your educational journey.

Contents

CONTENTS

Appendices

Please note the appendices can also be found in the eResources for this book at: www.routledge.com/9781138313842

Author Biography

Amy Bishop received a BSW from Northern Arizona University and an MSW from the University of Denver in 2004 with a focus in high-risk youth. While working for Adams County as an Educational Liaison, she helped to create the first Juvenile Justice Education Advocate position within Senate Bill 94 in the 17th Judicial District in 2007 and took the position herself in 2008. In addition, she conducts training and workshops nationwide on the educational needs of court-involved youth. She has worked as an Adjunct Professor for the University of Denver, Graduate School of Social Work, and has most recently completed the Georgetown University School to Justice Partnership Certificate program. She received the Division of Youth Services Significant Contribution Award in 2016. She also works as an Education Consultant for families, youth, schools, and agencies in improving educational outcomes.

Acknowledgments

Thanks to every individual working in this field who believed education should be a priority when planning for court-involved youth. In particular, my supervisor, Paul Targoff, who was not only my supervisor but a mentor in supporting me and agreeing that education was a priority for every County, not simply the one in which we designed the education advocate position. He was continually supportive in providing this information to others nationwide. Thank you, Paul, I am so lucky to have you as a mentor.

In addition, my sincere gratitude to the Douglas County Education Action Team, Pat Sweeney, Crystal Allen Ward, Georgetown University School to Justice Partnership, Andrea Skubal, and finally my parents, James and Rosemary Bishop, for your continued support and belief in my work.

Introduction to Framework

Chapter 1

Introduction

Educational aptitude and graduation rates continue to be an area for improvement for Colorado youth who encounter the child welfare and juvenile justice systems. Unfortunately, the decline in education and graduation is directly proportional to the barriers these youth face upon systems entry, which unnecessarily promotes recidivism. However, at the core of this issue is a prime opportunity for change that has shown effectiveness in Colorado. The change that is necessary to ensure our nation's court-involved youth have access to a brighter future is rooted in a collaborative approach to intervention in each community. Fortunately, this can be accomplished according to the needs in each community by utilizing existing resources and building on current initiatives. While this model was originally implemented in Colorado, its development is a compilation of the existing research across the country. Colorado is simply one of many states trying to improve educational outcomes for this population.

Though the educational gaps are countless, there are proven actions that can be taken within the existing system to improve strains on youth's success. At the core of these actions is collaboration. In examining a solution-based approach to improvement, it is difficult to ignore the recurring proposition that youth are better served through educational planning and advocacy when intervention is coordinated among the individual, family, and county levels. The US Departments of Education and Justice (2014) also state as a guiding principle that streamlining procedures to promote effectiveness across all systems is at the core of improving educational outcomes for court-involved youth. Furthermore, designing a system of shared information, vision, and efforts is most certainly one of the ways to not only improve academic outcomes but support youth's healthy growth into adulthood as well (Gonsoulin et al., 2012, p. I). However, as a nation, we are not doing this consistently. In a study of seven counties, results showed that not one "child welfare [agency] in any of the counties had developed a process for systematically sharing data about individual children with the schools in which the foster children were enrolled" (Leone & Weinberg, 2012, p. I9).

Founded on best practices in other states and within Colorado, this guide is a three-phase framework system that will aid in alleviating chronic barriers for youth. The guide combines the best practices and recommendations from national research with tactics that have been successfully employed in the field so it can be implemented in any community. Included are the necessary components to implement a collaborative, community-centered intervention system that effectively meets the needs of county, family, and individuals alike. With the understanding that each county carries its own strengths, barriers, and resources, the tools within this guide serve as a framework for assessing and creating an improved system that caters to the unique needs of each community in which it is implemented.

Well-known organizations such as National Technical Assistance Center for the Education of Neglected or Delinquent Children and Youth (NDTAC) indicate five guiding principles in supporting educational outcomes for court-involved youth, one of which is to establish procedures "through statutes, memoranda of understanding, and practices that ensure successful navigation across child serving systems and smooth reentry into communities" (Clark et al., 2013, p. 8). Furthermore, the recommendations include individualizing "system policies, programs and supervision to reflect the distinct developmental needs of adolescents" (p. 9). These recommendations align with the goals of this guide in that it is intentionally focused on adaptable tools to help create and/or improve procedures based on users' county and population needs. A study conducted in seven counties nationwide found that not one "child welfare [agency] in any of the counties had developed a process for systematically sharing data about individual children with the schools in which the foster children were enrolled" (Leone & Weinberg, 2012, p. 19). For juvenile justice youth, literature also indicates the need for consistent, dependable information sharing with schools (Gonsoulin et al., 2012).

It is important to acknowledge that many states across the country are attempting to address this urgent issue. However, many of the well-intended attempts to impact educational outcomes have failed because changes were implemented in silos. This type of response to the issue has a tendency to expose additional gaps and flaws, which forces further broad-scale examination of the issue as a result. For example, in Virginia, after enacting legislation to mandate the development of re-enrollment procedures, the education direct service was still not in place three years later, forcing the state to revisit the issue. As another instance, the state of California implemented the direct service Education Liaison position through AB490; however, communication and collaboration among agencies remained a barrier, prompting their current and subsequent efforts to move toward systemic changes that will address the resultant gaps in service across agencies (Leone & Weinberg, 2012). Such examples are numerous, so it is imperative to identify the underpinning needs of the system as a whole if the goal is to effect substantial and meaningful improvements in educational outcomes. In certain states, the issue of school discipline reform is addressed to help keep youth engaged in school with the intention of a preventative impact on youth not entering the court system as a result. States such as California, Illinois, Tennessee, Connecticut, and North Carolina saw major reductions in school suspensions as a result of their reform measures (Council of State Governments Justice Center, 2017). This is still only one system creating change and is not the entire solution to this multi-faceted systemic problem.

In other states, such as Louisiana, there is an established re-entry program, yet there is no report of the type of services offered prior to commitment. This is common in re-entry programs across the country; a much higher degree of importance is placed on transition services for youth who are leaving a long-term commitment facility than for court-involved youth who are transitioning between community schools (Louisiana Partnership for Children and Families, 2015). When transition planning is not to the forefront, agencies have a propensity to work at odds, lacking clarity on respective responsibilities and which agency is taking the lead on educational planning. To further complicate matters, transition planning upon release from detention, treatment placements, or corrections has an unnecessarily high potential of incompliance with court requirements for youth to enroll/attend school, as schools will often prohibit enrollment or not have the appropriate program for the youth to earn a diploma. Often times, if agencies and schools are not coordinating, high school age youth are released during inappropriate times during a school term. This ultimately ends in the youth sitting out of school awaiting enrollment after release from any facility (Roy-Stevens, 2004). This guide proposes not waiting until a juvenile justice youth is committed but rather begin educational services at the forefront of system entry to keep youth engaged in school rather than re-engage them later and provide equivalent prevention for child welfare as well. It is theorized that if systems give the proper attention to academic standing initially, it may prevent any future educational barriers. As the Graduation Alliance (2015) has stated in their token phrase, "make it harder to leave and easier to return" (p. 1). National research suggests that up to $60,000 is spent per year for youth in commitment, whereas it only costs $7,000 yearly to educate a youth in a community school (Stephens & Arnette, 2000). This financial difference alone is enough to encourage state agencies to partner with school districts upfront on all child welfare and juvenile justice cases to prevent further systems involvement and simultaneously improve graduation rates.

Chapter 2

System Barriers to Success

There are well-known barriers to success, highlighting the need for a streamlined approach to educational planning. Poor educational outcomes are the result of lacking prevention and intervention services among agencies and schools working with youth. Lack of prevention for child welfare youth occurs because best interest determinations are not considered consistently in the start of a case nor with each residential or facility move. Lack of prevention is also evident in the lack of academic monitoring once a youth is court-involved, particularly for general education students where there is not a documented special education Individualized Education Plan (IEP) to follow a youth in multiple settings or to simply provide documented support for youth in the home school while experiencing out of home placement or juvenile justice involvement. Child welfare youth might enter the system doing well in school, but outside circumstances can quickly lead to academic decline. However, systems are not taking that into consideration when a case opens. Ideally, if a youth is thriving in a school, regardless of residential instability, all efforts would be made to help the youth stay successful in school, thus increasing likelihood of graduation. Fostering Success in Education: National Factsheet (2014) cited a national study of 1,087 foster care alum and found youth who had even one fewer change in living situation per year were almost twice as likely to graduate from high school before leaving foster care. While the Every Student Succeeds Act of 2015 (ESSA) Best Interest Determination mandates are a great start, a youth still needs academic support while experiencing child welfare involvement, similar to a youth needing mental health supports and/or other services to ensure well-being. In Colorado, the amount of County Education Coordinators in child welfare facilitating Best Interest Determination (BID) meetings are increasing; however, those positions are not required to provide education direct service to ensure youth continue to progress academically after a placement decision is made.

Risk of Crossover Youth

This lack of prevention and intervention can potentially contribute to a child welfare youth becoming involved in the juvenile justice system, particularly if the youth disengages from school. In recent years, crossover youth status has received more attention while national research shows that 65% of youth involved in the juvenile justice system were once or are currently also in the child welfare system (Griller Clark et al., 2016). At this point, once youth are involved in multiple systems, they are at higher risk of the systemic barriers such as high mobility in placements, falling behind academically, being labeled a "bad kid," or being automatically filtered into an alternative school. The literature cites the "relationship between maltreatment, delinquency and educational problems is well documented and complex" (Abbott & Barnett, 2016, p. 4). Moreover, a study by Baglivio et al. (2016), Maltreatment, Child Welfare, and Recidivism in a Sample of Deep End Crossover Youth, further highlights the need for all systems including education to work more collaboratively to mitigate the negative impact of crossover youth status. Juvenile justice youth face additional unique barriers such as a troubled home environment, negative reputation in community or school, negative peer associations, financial struggles, and frequent hardship understanding the systems in which they are obligated to comply (Farn & Adams, 2016). This is an ongoing issue nationwide as programs such as The Crossover Youth Practice Model have emerged in efforts to adequately meet the needs of this population (Farn & Adams, 2016). Even without child welfare involvement initially, youth who become entrenched in the justice system often experience lack of school engagement for many years before ever committing a crime that may lead to child welfare involvement later. This further justifies the need to include the school as an equal partner the moment a youth becomes systems involved, as they may have extensive information and background on youth that is beneficial for outside agencies. Likewise, agencies may have extensive family history that would benefit schools to understand. This partnership and information sharing can lead to an enhanced understanding of youth that has the potential of changing the approach for working with them in various settings.

Lack of Coordination Between Agencies and Schools in Educational Planning

Coordination occurs not only at the systemic level in which policies and procedures are defined but at the direct service level. Much of the research in the last ten years recommends that local agencies seek out partnerships with the school districts to collaborate on continuous enrollment strategies and coordinate on tactics to reduce learning barriers. When direct service staff are interviewed to determine gaps in service, reports often include ongoing issues related to information sharing and records transfer—both of which have severe consequences to the youth, ranging from short-term minor disruptions in enrollment to long-term problems associated with prolonged school absences, severed peer relationships, misplaced service interventions, and so on. Baglivio et al. (2016) recommends formally creating protocols, staff training, and measures of performance. Cross-agency coordination and collaboration are key elements to preventing undue consequences for the youth while they are involved with system interventions. Although educational planning is often not specifically addressed, it is an essential component of youth-centered services. Effectiveness with collaborative models has also been shown to strengthen partnerships between juvenile justice and school districts in various counties, further supporting the proposition to implement education planning specifically in a similar fashion.

Agencies have an opportunity to improve graduation rates among academically disadvantaged youth involved in juvenile justice by providing appropriate educational planning and supports, which aids in preparing the youth for leading productive adult lives. Many studies show youth often outgrow criminal behaviors, but involvement in juvenile justice proportionally correlates to declines in long-term academic achievement and employment success. This general trend in youth behavior also supports the cross-system collaborative model among justice and education systems stakeholders, also suggesting there may also be significant potential of prevention if collaborative efforts aim to reduce juvenile justice referrals and promote school enrollment and achievement (Seigle et al., 2014). As most systems currently operate, education is the last piece of the planning puzzle and often an afterthought. While countless committees include child welfare, probation, courts, and mental health, the local school district is often overlooked as a standard representative of these groups. The downfall of such an oversight is that discussions and plans are made irrespective of school district policies and procedures, therefore, devoid of an essential component. The fallout is that the school district is perceived to be the barrier, though it was not provided an option to be part of a solution.

High Rates of Dropout Due to School Instability

Juvenile Justice/Crossover Youth

In Colorado, graduation rates are not available for juvenile justice involved youth as the state does not collect this information. It is documented that only 40% of states track a youth's enrollment into an educational program and even less track GED enrollment post-commitment making it impossible to accurately report graduation rates for juvenile justice youth. Though there are similarities among outcomes for child welfare and juvenile justice youth, there are also issues unique to juvenile justice and crossover youth who are arrested and placed in detention. For these youth in particular, this is an unavoidable transition that must be adequately addressed. Given the statistics on school mobility, it is known that juvenile justice youth suffer with each school move as well and are, on average with minimal moves, two years behind academically as compared with non-court-involved peers (Osher et al., 2012). In addition, youth in juvenile justice can experience stays in detention facilities lasting anywhere from 0 to beyond 60 days while awaiting court decisions, which significantly disrupts school progress.

It is known from the literature that 60% of prison inmates are without a high school education and school plays a major role in a person's future (NEA, 2013). It is also well known that "enrollment in school and academic achievement is associated with lower rates of reoffending and better outcomes into adulthood, and degree attainment is strongly associated with future earning potential" (Seigle et al., 2014, p. 69). Finally, most youth "age out" of delinquent behavior whether they are caught or not. Even the majority of youth who commit serious offenses cease all criminal activity by young adulthood, yet many of these youth report struggling to gain academic success after veering off track. For this reason, it behooves the entire community to offer a supportive network of opportunity to reconnect youth to community schools to successfully graduate high school. These youth are our future workforce and will need an education to pursue employment successfully thus making the education stability for juvenile justice youth of particular importance.

Furthermore, Colorado does not require a specialist specifically coordinating education transition from short-term detention stays. Youth are withdrawn from the home school and an enrollment transfer occurs to the detention center in the school district; although options for a parent/guardian to collect schoolwork for youth while in they are in detention are not typically discussed. It is an automatic assumption that youth will be enrolled and attend detention school. With the many online schooling options and access to school online platforms, it is feasible that a youth could do work for home school while in detention. As it stands currently, youth may spend weeks in detention; fall behind in home school workload, detention center seat hours do not transfer appropriately, and youth ultimately fails an entire school term. Even more concerning is the lack of education transition specialists for longer stays after a commitment to correctional facilities nationwide. In 2015, it was reported that only 11 states have specific education liaisons facilitating transition.

Research shows that school disciplinary actions, including out of school suspension and expulsion, prior to incarceration also contribute to academic delays by interrupting educational time in the classroom. This highlights an additional area for concern and further emphasizes the need to promote educational stability and develop prevention tactics through school culture and disciplinary measures that allow youth to remain in the classroom.

In Colorado, Advancing the Colorado Graduates Agenda, Mac Iver et al. (2009) addressed the dropout problem for the general population. Specifically, it recommends completely reforming truancy and attendance policies around early intervention so warning behaviors trigger prevention tactics that are enforced for the entire school. While schools may attempt a phased approach to implementing these policy recommendations, the authors suggest a systemic approach so all changes occur at once. The recommendation for a comprehensive approach to change is in direct alignment with this guide's framework, which addresses all levels of service simultaneously. Though the guide is highly specific and targets court-involved youth, its use promises a more effective approach to lowering dropout totals than the piecemeal efforts to date.

Child Welfare Youth

It is widely known among professionals associated with child welfare services that youth placed in out-of-home care experience, on average, one to two residential placement changes per year, and each move to a new school causes the youth to fall behind academically by four to six months. Studies show sustained enrollment and high school attendance to be extremely important to preventing dropout and avoiding course failure. It was recorded in a study in 2009 that only about 30% of Colorado child welfare youth graduate (Clemens & Sheesley, 2016) and this is often due to the number of school moves a youth experiences.

A study out of Chicago of high school freshman students reported, "only 63% of students who missed about one week of school graduated in four years" (p. 6). Furthermore, it was proven that "attendance is clearly a vital part of graduating ... but beyond this we show evidence later ... that attendance and continuous enrollment is the most essential requirement for avoiding course failure" (Allensworth & Easton, 2007, p. 6). In a study of foster care youth in Illinois conducted by Chapin Hall Center for Children, information was recorded to further support improving educational outcomes of child welfare youth. Findings showed that "students in care who are dropping out of school between the ages 13 and 16 is more than double the averages for other students in the [Chicago Public Schools] system" (Skyles, Smithgall, & Howard, 2007, p. 2). The authors noted that the failure to transition from middle school to high school was an indicator of early dropout age as well. Balfanz (2007) identifies four classic reasons for dropout among all youth, which should be considered for court-involved youth, including: life events that occur outside of the classroom; fade outs present with boredom or frustration due to lacking attention from parents/guardians; push outs exhibiting disciplinary issues and perceived threats; and failures to succeed caused by unmet environmental needs in the home and at school (p. 3). Both child welfare and juvenile justice youth can struggle with every single one of these barriers simultaneously, while some non-court-involved youth may only exhibit one barrier and still dropout. Hence, one can only imagine how much more intense negative educational experiences must be for court-involved youth.

Recently, Colorado began reporting on graduation and mobility rates for foster care students. It is only in the last few years that the low graduation rate has become an urgent concern for state officials. According to the Colorado Department of Education Fact Sheet on foster care education in 2015, less than 70% of foster care youth finish high school before leaving the child welfare system. Furthermore, statistics from 2013 indicate only one of every three Colorado students placed in foster care during high school graduated within the standard four years (Clemens, 2014). In Colorado, foster care youth have a mobility rate of 54%, whereas the state mobility average for all youth is only 16.5%. As previously noted, youth in foster care also show a significant decrease in graduation rates at 30% whereas the state average graduation rate is 77.3%.

Nationwide studies now show that the education students receive in residential facilities may not be equivalent to education in a public school setting (American Youth Forum, 2018). Aside from inconsistencies in educational standards, there also lacks consistency in transporting youth to the home school while in placement in a residential facility. Without consideration of such incongruence, youth are set up for educational deficiencies upon re-entry to the community school, further complicating the dropout epidemic. The opportunity to avoid this problem has always been within reasonable expectation of agencies and schools but not considered consistently. Not only is it possible but now it is required at the national level. Negative educational outcomes for youth involved in child welfare is receiving attention and there are now mandates for child welfare youth to remain in the home school with viable transportation provided until a best interest determination meeting occurs and future academic placement is assessed. This should include facility placements as well. The fundamental truth within this new law is that youth perform better with even one less academic change in placement. Establishing this systemic procedure is addressed, in detail, in the phase 2 of this guide.

Lack of Educational Planning
Direct Service and Support

As stated previously, many juvenile justice youth have a history of school issues, yet supports and interventions that properly address the areas of need are severely lacking. Even if a youth only has one charge and is seemingly performing well at intake, immediate attention to education is of utmost importance to prevent academic decline. Outside agencies often give attention to education when a youth is already in a large academic deficit or has stopped attending entirely. It is far more difficult to re-engage a youth than to keep a youth engaged in school. When we have to rely on re-engagement of a youth, we are often looking at a need for academic, "programming at different levels of intensity, available in a variety of locations, and delivered through different institutional arrangements and blends of supports and opportunities" (Allen et al., 2004, p. 5). Those of which are often not available to youth in certain school districts, particularly those without proper funding or smaller rural communities.

Youth returning from residential facilities are placed in remedial classes at the high school level and often need individual tutoring and support when in public school to perform at grade level. Due to the lack of academic equality, studies repeatedly report that court-involved youth tend to experience high levels of grade retention compared with their non-court-involved peers. More importantly, in a study of incarcerated youth, 60% report repeating a grade (Council of State Governments, 2017). As a result, they are more likely to be over age for their grade and under credited as compared with peers of the same age and uninvolved in court systems. Ideally, individual education planning would be a standard of support for all court-involved youth.

It was only in 2007 that the 17th Judicial District saw this need and created an education direct service position and it was the first of its kind in Colorado. In 2015, of the total number of youth who were receiving services from the Senate Bill 94 Educational Advocate and successfully termed as "enrolled and attending" school at the time of closure, only 23% of these youth recidivated as compared with the 37% of youth who recidivated and did not receive services from the Educational Advocate. One might say that direct educational service planning was a contributing factor leading to a successful exit out of the juvenile justice system. More significant outcomes are seen in Washington where a statewide Education Advocate program is in place that broadly demonstrated a lower rate of recidivism and higher academic outcomes among youth involved in the program. Washington reported that, of the 78 youth in the program, 91% of them did not recidivate (EA Evaluation Report, 2016), reinforcing a strong correlation between improving educational outcomes to reduce rates of recidivism.

As previously mentioned, in both Maine and Washington, individual youth are assigned educational liaisons and advocates to provide direct educational planning. Overall, research shows that regardless of the type of individual direct service support provided, whether it is mentoring, advocacy, tutoring, or coaching, any level of positive adult connection and/or support has substantial impact on educational outcomes. Conversely, in Colorado and the majority of states across the US, individual services are not consistently provided and educational planning for court-involved youth is, paradoxically, completed as a reactionary measure. While the implementation of an education advocacy program is effective, as noted in the ESD 112 EA evaluation report, the majority of stakeholders also reported increased collaboration among systems as a way to improve educational outcomes as well. This further supports that direct service, while crucial, should be done in conjunction with systems change.

Lack of Education Transition Planning

One important piece to educational stability is establishing smooth educational transition protocols for any school move. Clemens and Sheesley (2016) noted, and this guide concurs, that for youth, "every school transition – not just those associated with child welfare placement changes – counts" (p. 1). Furthermore, while making recommendations of continuity of care in academics while youth transition schools, these authors found there not to be, "a packaged and tested approach available to fully meet this goal" (p. 23), which this guide seeks to remedy by providing an all-encompassing detailed framework that was implemented in practice. Within the juvenile justice system, the literature suggests a consistent struggle in the ability to transition youth into public school (Siegle et al., 2014, The Council of State Governments, 2017). This is detrimental to a youth when education momentum is gained in a facility as it is known that "when incarcerated youth are productively engaged in educational programming, they tend to experience fewer disciplinary problems in school and throughout the juvenile facility" (Leone & Weinberg, 2012, p. 20). This is certainly a characteristic worth maintaining as a youth transitions into the community, yet many are not doing so effectively. As a result, "as many as two-thirds of youth fail to reenroll in school after returning from confinement, and those youth who are not attached to school upon release are more likely to drop out and reoffend" (The National Evaluation and Technical Assistance Center, 2011, p. 32). In addition, uncoordinated planning leads to unclear responsibilities, communication barriers, variable levels of staff commitment, and failure in records transfer processes. Transition teams can better support youth by focusing on planning that sustains momentum gained in residential care in terms of sobriety, mental health, and academic progress. Lacking a clear coordinated education transition has high potential to thwart the youth's progress and positive momentum, risking academic engagement altogether.

Streamlining procedures between all of these systems is an absolute necessity to ensure proper education stability planning for youth. According to Gomperts (2014), "students leave school not because of a particular event or factor but because circumstances accumulate in ways that push school further and further down their list of priorities" (p. 6). Many young foster youth experience overwhelming risk factors early in life and agencies can coordinate with schools to mitigate these factors. Furthermore, many of these circumstantial barriers accumulate with multiple transitions in and out of community schools leaving no time to build lasting school connections. At the child welfare level, Casey Family Programs (2004) noted "special education systems and the child welfare agencies do a poor job of working together seamlessly to prepare youth to move into adult living" (p. 35), an essential goal in proper education planning not only for special education but general education youth as well. This lack of collaboration is evident at every level of system involvement, including school transitions even though the literature repeatedly makes the recommendation. In the Transition Toolkit 2.0 by Brock et al. (2008), three concepts are identified as key elements in successful transitions. These include coordination, outcome focused procedures, and supporting transition success. The toolkit also supports the assignment of a single point of contact to coordinate transition and clear identification of roles of other agencies, schools, and families. Shifting these recommendations into action may make the difference in youth recidivism, academic stability, and educational achievement. For juvenile justice youth, there are many states that provide a detailed transition procedure from commitment to community that includes mental health, employment, community engagement, and education. However, youth may experience multiple transitions prior to commitment that are often overlooked and unplanned. More specifically, for these multiple transitions, this means that the school should have a point of contact for this purpose, individual school staff should be included in youth team, and transition timing should stay in line as closely as possible with school calendars particularly for adolescent youth working toward a credit-based diploma.

Gagnon and Richards (2008) identified five major guideposts that were meant to improve transition outcomes for juvenile justice youth. These guideposts are similar to what child welfare youth need for successful transitions as well. These guideposts include "school-based preparatory experiences, career preparation, youth development in leadership, community activities, and family involvement" (p. 13). More specifically, guidepost #1: School based preparatory experiences include education transition recommendations for youth stepping down out of residential facilities back into community schools. The guideposts suggest successful outcomes are dependent on facility schools meeting the state academic requirements for curriculum and qualified staff. However, this is a nationwide problem, and many states are not yet meeting that standard consistently. The 2013–2014 reports from the US Department of Education show that facilities are also providing fewer seat hours toward education and fewer core classes than community schools around the country. As a result, the educational transition support that professionals provide youth must compensate for the possibility that a youth is below grade level. This is why it is so important to have all agencies participate in educational planning. More specifically, outside agencies can provide funding for tutoring and mentoring, two services that are often necessary when compensating for academic deficit. When educational planning is on the forefront of a case, workers can quickly identify any necessary academic support upon transition at monthly staffing meetings throughout youth placement. Proactive assessment assures that the receiving school district has the information needed to prepare supports and aid in a successful return to the community school.

There is not much research is available of examples of streamlined academic transition procedures in child welfare. Fundamentally, such a significant gap in service places great value in this guide, as it contains the tools necessary to enables professionals in educational settings to create procedures within the current system. When systems are not aligned in transitional procedures and information sharing, it increases the difficulty for youth experiencing multiple school settings. Planning for education transition thus becomes crucial if a youth cannot avoid school moves. All systems and youth stand to benefit from action team collaboration to ensure supports are in place for any type of transition.

The tools and recommendations in this guide put educational planning at the forefront of residential placement as well. This framework aligns with the most recent research recommending that transition planning begins the moment a youth enters a facility (Brock, O'Cummings, & Milligan, 2008). It is centered on youth and family goals, which also empowers the parent to contribute to transition details and the plan's success.

Chapter 3

Individual Barriers to Success

All too often, court-involved youth experience individual barriers to educational success. The barriers often range from child abuse/neglect, educational instability, trauma-impacting learning, parental neglect of education, challenging behaviors, learning disabilities, truancy, suspensions, and expulsions. In addition to the barriers presented with discipline, lack of academic skill, grade-level retention, and learning disabilities, existence of internal barriers must also be acknowledged (Council of State Governments Justice Center, 2013). While addressing the areas of concern for systems reform, the mental and emotional state of youth deserves equal attention, as the youth psyche can contribute to barriers and struggles in the general education classroom regardless of how well the systems coordinate. By partnering with school districts, systems will find it easier to provide training and collaborative supports to more appropriately handle at-risk youth challenges in the classroom.

Court-involved youth often have a traumatic history of events that directly impact their ability to function appropriately in a learning environment. Such issues are often discounted as they tend to manifest in the classroom with behaviors that mimic Attention-Deficit Hyperactivity Disorder (ADHD) or Conduct Disorder, particularly as youth age and do not receive proper support for their academic needs. The most common characteristics that prove to be the largest barriers include inability to communicate needs, organize thoughts, focus on classroom materials and instruction, interact with peers, self-regulate emotions, comply with classroom conduct, and control impulses and anger (Cole et al., 2005). This further indicates the need for cross-agency training and direct service individuals who aim to understand the root of these emotional and behavioral issues with consideration of youth history, triggers, and academic need. It is also noted that a "school setting can be a battleground in which traumatized children's assumptions of the world as a dangerous place sabotage their ability to develop constructive relationships with nurturing adults" (Cole et al., 2005), making it difficult for educators and administrators who do not understand the internal struggle of a traumatized youth. If the relevant educators have the appropriate background information on court-involved youth, they could be apt to address the behavior through a more productive approach rather than extreme disciplinary measures. There is an urgent need to ensure trauma-informed care is integrated in the educational planning process when youth are involved in court systems. Furthermore, "maltreated youth have evidenced delinquency rates 47% greater than youth without at least one substantiated maltreatment allegation" (Baglivio et al., 2016, p. 2), thus indicating that trauma history is a significant factor in working with court-involved youth. Compounding individuals' internal struggles with uncoordinated systems and services, the educational barriers for youth become insurmountable for a majority and the remaining minority struggles through the disjointed system to defy the odds and graduate high school.

Though a multitude of barriers can culminate in a perfect storm for these adolescents, phase 3 of this guide addresses academic mindsets, internal motivations, and personal goals. Phase 3 will provide guidance on how individual and education direct service staff can consistently learn more about students' learning needs and barriers that will help build a supportive academic environment for the student to thrive.

Chapter 4

Relevance of County Guide

This three-phase framework addresses the key recommendations from the most significant studies related to improving educational outcomes within the last ten years, including but not limited to:

- Sharing information on youth's involvement in each system to coordinate interventions;
- Partner with education system;
- Data sharing across systems;
- Establishment of formal protocols and processes across systems;
- Formation of a formal committee/structure that meets regularly to coordinate efforts in improving educational outcomes;
- Collaborated goals and indicators of success in addition to an action plan for committee; and
- Utilize data and outcomes to guide policy, practice, and resource allocation.
(Brock et al., 2008)

Studies continue to show that "enrollment in school and academic achievement is associated with lower rates of reoffending and better outcomes into adulthood, and degree attainment is strongly associated with future earning potential" (Seigle et al., 2014, p. 37). However, the collaboration necessary to improve enrollment and academic achievement is often lacking. National organizations dedicated to juvenile justice reform efforts repeatedly recommend that local juvenile justice agencies should seek out the partnership with school districts to keep students enrolled continuously, assist in reforming discipline efforts, and coordinate approaches to addressing barriers to learning (Farn & Adams 2016). Griller Clark et al. (2016) remarked that nationwide, "while there are attempts to address and connect services to meet the needs of these youth prior to, during, and after secure care, in general, there is lack of awareness and communication and a duplication of efforts" (p. 7). Within the Crossover Youth Model (2013) it is stated that "school representatives must be part of the team of people planning for and supporting youth development" (p. 85). It goes on to say that school staff must also be fully informed of the youth's system status to truly understand the range of academic needs. Title I, Part D funding is widely available to support these efforts and should be considered when using this guide framework, particularly for the implementation of phase 3. More specifically, the funds are available to, "help youth meet statewide academic standards; prevent schools from pushing youth out of school and into the juvenile justice system; facilitate youth's transition from facilities to further education or employment through additional requirements around the transfer of student records and course credits" (Council of State Governments, 2018, p. 3).

For child welfare youth specifically, implications for practice from Rubin et al. (2013) provided in the report on *Improving Education Outcomes for Children in Child Welfare*, included recommendations for action including "promote real time data sharing and communication across to systems to support collaborative, child level case management ... systemically track and respond to school absences and ... integrate the delivery of education, child welfare and behavioral health services" (p. 1). These guide recommendations are in agreement that coordinating systems upfront (phase 1 and 2) establishes more effective coordination of individual workers at the direct service level (phase 3). This report further noted that professionals nationwide are struggling with the same types of systems issues that are faced in Colorado, such as a lack of cross-agency collaboration and an unclear understanding of roles and polices not only within their own agency but understanding outside organizations as well. While some of the national recommendations are difficult for some due to financial or political reasons, this guide only takes dedication and commitment to improving outcomes to see success. Overall, it is well recognized that creative coordination of systems and education is necessary to improve educational outcomes.

Engagement in education is a top protective factor to prevent recidivism and it is important to future success for foster care students once they leave the child welfare system. As a result, it benefits county professionals to utilize this framework to promote a paradigm shift within agencies and consider school staff an equal partner to ensure educational stability is at the forefront of every client case plan. This guide will not only address the systematic paradigm shift that must occur to improve outcomes but also the direct service addition in procedures necessary to promote educational success at the start of every case.

County Guide Framework in Action

Senate Bill 94 within Colorado is designed to provide the Judicial District specifically tailored funding for juvenile services to maintain youth in the community safely. The Senate Bill 94 Coordinator then has the ability to design a budget specific to Judicial District needs and resources. In the 17th Judicial District, the Senate Bill 94 program houses an Education Advocate specifically designed to provide direct educational planning for juveniles and crossover youth. This includes collaborating with schools and agencies in creating educational plans that address youth's individualized educational needs. This was the first county in Colorado to create such a position. The author of this guide is one of the creators of the Education Advocate position in partnership with the Senate Bill 94 Coordinator. The author created all of the policies and procedures for this position which are enhanced in this guide to show what is truly possible to achieve in phase 3 Interventions.

In Douglas County, Colorado, the Educational Action Team is in place to implement the framework described in this guide with the involvement of many major government agencies with the local school district. In partnership with this author, the team first established standardized procedures for best interest determinations and educational planning for foster youth and implemented an Educational Navigator direct service position. In 2017, a subcommittee was created for juvenile justice and a school district partnership to review current school discipline practices and keeping youth engaged in school. The action team is overseen by the Douglas County Human Services Program Development Manager, meets once a month, and continues to improve systems procedures in maintaining educational stability across all systems for youth.

Chapter 5

Organization of Guide

Three-Phase Framework (County, Systems, Individual)

This guide encompasses a three-phase framework that effectively addresses all gaps and barriers youth encounter in the journey toward educational success. Phase I is designed to address county level barriers. These barriers can range from lack of communication of multiple agencies, formal information sharing, and formal processes when planning for education for court-involved youth. The guide framework targets identified to be most impactful in educational stability and outcomes for court-involved youth are stratified by county, systems, and individual levels and they are defined as follows:

Phase I County: A framework for creating an Education Action Team that specializes in cross-agency collaboration, establishing roles within agencies and teams, identifying focus areas, and garnering agreements to facilitate changes within respective agencies. At the county level, the aim is to collectively target systemic gaps in educational stability and barriers specific to the county so educational outcomes of court-involved youth are directly impacted. The county-level collaboration naturally addresses the barrier of records transfer accountability as processes outlined will automatically trigger the transfer of records. It is well known that transferring youth records is crucial in keeping education continuous (Griller Clark et al., 2016).

It is suggested there exists five major goals that are the key to improving outcomes, which are in line with the creation of an Education Action Team described in phase I. These include:

The establishment of a formal ongoing structure for collaboration;
  Identification of shared goals and indicators of success;
  Devise an action plan to achieve these goals;
  Establish data/records sharing and other cross systems protocols
and processes;
  Facilitate regular cross agency training;
  Evaluate outcomes, and share and use data to guide improvements.
                                                    (Seigle et al., 2014, p. 69)

Phase 2 Systems: A framework for cross-agency training development and collaboration among systems at the level of direct services. In phase 2, the framework includes possible position responsibilities for the Child Welfare Education Liaison or other school point of contact and the roles that other professionals play within an individual case. Phase 2 builds on utilizing the notification procedure and specific educational points of contact within each agency. Finally, this phase encompasses educational transitions as it involves many different systems working collaboratively to educationally plan for youth.

Phase 3 Individual: Provides a framework for all direct service procedures and protocols for a liaison, advocate, navigator, and/or other service provider involved in educational intake, planning, and record keeping. Once the systems are effectively implementing standards of procedures as a result of phase 2, the direct service staff working with youth are able to pay more attention to individual academic needs.

Included in phase 3 are sample documents such as an educational intake form, enrollment checklist, transition summary, and numerous other documents that can be used in the field. The new direct service positions can tailor these documents to work within the new system most effectively. Phase 3 builds on procedures implemented in phase 1 and 2, thus allowing individual youth teams to effectively identify individual barriers such as motivation, trauma impacting academics, learning deficits, and numerous other factors impacting the youth's ability to be successful in the classroom.

Chapter 6

Using This Guide

As described previously, this guide is formatted into a three-phase framework. This design serves as a reference point for each level of service that must be addressed in order for educational outcomes to improve. In order to achieve the most impact on educational outcomes, change in processes must happen not only at the county and systems level but at the individual level as well. While these levels are outlined sequentially, many of the interventions can be done simultaneously. The action team may find they are implementing components of each level of service in the first year and this will work as long as the county and smaller systems involved are collaborating effectively and are specifically designing processes to include individual level services.

In the first year of implementation, Douglas County not only implemented a school district notification process of child welfare involvement for the School District Child Welfare Education Liaison (CWEL) but also created a subcommittee to address school intervention and discipline frameworks beginning with one high school. Finally, in that first year, Douglas County Human Services, with the support of the action team, created an education direct service position of Educational Navigator. As a result, the Douglas County Education Action Team worked on three main goals for the first year that incorporated one goal from each phase.

It is encouraged that professionals come together to implement the phase I action team first and foremost with focus groups as a first step before creating an action plan for the first year. After the action team has fully implemented the initial steps in phase I, they can then incorporate goals from different phases.

It is often critical to bring in an outside facilitator and/or consultant to convene and effectively organize an Education Action Team. This person will direct the process via the County Guide and keep the process of change moving forward. This person can also be the educational staff hired to provide direct service, a judge, magistrate, or the child welfare or juvenile services staff that initiated the implementation of the guide. However, it is important to consider beneficial factors of an outside consultant including, "bringing new perspectives to old problems, asking questions that on one inside the organization is able to, providing crucial additional resources, acting as a sounding board, independence from the organization power structure and acting as a catalyst for change to happen" as indicated in the *Guidebook for Juvenile Justice & Child Welfare System Coordination and Integration* (Wiig et al., 2013, p. 26).

The designer of this framework is available for consultation at a variety of levels allowing for proper and individualized implementation for each action team. Individualized training for action teams are also available to help organize and implement all three phases. See www.educationstabilityconsultant.com for more information.

Guide Implementation Components

The following key components summarize a full implementation of the County Guide. It is a final list of components, that once implemented, show successful collaboration of the Education Action Team. By implementing all three phases; action teams will achieve the following:

- The creation of a clear mission statement of the Education Action Team;
- Action team members committed to bringing educational planning proce-dures to their respective agencies;
- Identified county specific educational gaps in service for court-involved youth;
- Clear picture of educational current procedures and specific identified points of change to insert educational planning at the forefront of each case;
- Consistent school district notification of court involvement procedures;
- Consistent immediate exchange and transfer of general and special educa-tion records;
- Implementation of a sustainable action team long term with policies on updated points of contact when a team member leaves their position;
- Review and establishment of information sharing across systems;
- Established key points of contact through action team commitment;
- Established cross-agency training and a regular training schedule;
- Creation and follow through of three goals each year to improve educa-tional outcomes;
- Establishment of Best Interest Determination protocol and training to cre-ate awareness and sustain new changes in processes;
- Written policies and procedures for people providing educational direct service; and
- Written policies and procedures for the school district CWEL or other school point of contact in coordination with new educational planning pro-cedures of outside agencies.

Phase 1

County Interventions

Chapter 7

Phase 1 Introduction

Why an Action Team?

Creating a team committed to improving educational outcomes repeatedly emerges as one of the most effective ways to create and sustain change. One of the largest barriers occurs when professionals are not aligned in their practices. For example, within juvenile justice, Seigle et al (2014) reports:

> Most juvenile justice systems acknowledge the importance of this collaboration, but they also fail to commit to its implementation. Instead, juvenile justice systems are often left to tackle challenges such as arranging for school enrollment or connecting youth with appropriate mental health services on a case-by-case basis. As a result, reducing recidivism and other positive youth outcomes are often heavily dependent on local receptivity to systems collaboration, the existence of cross systems protocols, and the willingness of specific public agency staff to return phone calls or attend meetings.
>
> (p. 69)

With the implementation of a formal Education Action Team, systems will avoid this common barrier to effective planning. Furthermore, literature suggests that systems of shared responsibility is indeed a way to foster not only improved educational outcomes but the general health of youth as well (Gonsoulin et al, 2012). Moreover, "a collaborative approach to service delivery is not just a good idea; it is the only way to do business if we are sincere about improving the dismal outcomes experienced by many of these youth" (Leone & Weinberg, 2012, p. 41). The Education Action Team framework described below targets all of the collaborative needs simultaneously not only for juvenile justice youth but for child welfare youth as well. Often, the same agencies are involved in both child welfare and juvenile justice cases and information sharing required for the educational planning for both populations will require a similar set of procedure implementations.

Collaboration leads to:

- Less duplication of efforts and systems working at odds with one another;
- Streamlined court, agency, and provider decision making and service delivery;
- Increased utilization of available services and an identification of service gaps so juvenile justice and other service systems can cost effectively address the needs of youth across systems;
- Developmentally appropriate educational planning;
- Trauma informed academic care, planning and support.

Since systems typically operate independently, the most effective service is delivered in states whose agencies understand how each system works, where they overlap, and what aspects are supporting or hindering youth. For example, the aforementioned Nevada Student Attendance and Disturbance Committee comprised of state and local education and judicial leaders focus on attendance and discipline issues across the state. As members continued their collaboration they saw the need for cross-agency training and learned from each other how to best coordinate educational efforts. It is a continued concern from all government agencies that, "philosophical, structural, language, and communication barriers prevent agencies from forming partnerships" (Gonsoulin et al., 2012, p. 1). In some cases, this manifests as staff perceiving an increase in workload and we must counteract that concern. Furthermore, "it is not uncommon for organizations to have deeply entrenched (and sometimes inaccurate) beliefs about systems partners, a significant investment in their current way of functioning, and skepticism about the value of new endeavors that require time and resources" (Wiig et al., 2013, p. 3). Despite any push back from local agencies and/or schools, it is important to push the education agenda forward and establish the action team. The initiator of this team must find committed leadership, valuable stakeholders committed to the cause, and sustain ongoing communication and action of the shared vision within the team. The initiator must also be mindful of approaching all agencies and schools from a shared vision of wanting to improve educational outcomes in an open and honest forum within the action team. It must be communicated that the team will work to break down systems barriers, increase cross systems communication and collaboration, and clarify roles of educational planning regardless of any seemingly uncooperative experiences.

Phase 1 Key Terms

Education Action Team: Team of agency members committing to the cause both within the respective agency and within the team to assist in the actions necessary to improve educational outcomes for court-involved youth.

Focus Groups: Action Team members coming together to pinpoint specific gaps in services that are barriers in improving educational outcomes for court-involved youth.

Point of Contact: Shall be known herein as "POC." The purpose of a point of contact is to streamline the process of notification of involvement, information sharing, records exchanges, and consistent immediate communication establishment between systems.

Champion or Leader of Action Team: The initiator in the county who commits to creating and sustaining the County Education Action Team.

Education Direct Service Staff: Any education staff providing individual direct educational planning for youth is known herein as "ES." This might be an Educational Advocate, Navigator, Liaison, or the like.

17th JD Education Advocate: This is an ES position created by Senate Bill 94 Coordinator and Amy Bishop in 2008. Amy Bishop developed the procedures for this position and the direct service in this guide builds on those original procedures. It serves as an example of how a county might develop and/or adapt county ES position.

Examples of Collaboration Nationwide

The need for a specific team to target improving educational outcomes is evident nationwide as many counties throughout the country have created collaborative groups similar to an Education Action Team. These teams are organized, sustainable, and create real change in the county. It is recommended that the team meets regularly, develop an action plan with goals, tasks, timelines, and identify roles within agencies to ensure continual improvement. The hiring of a coordinator to facilitate the team activities and functions is often necessary and initial team members should decide this jointly. It is suggested that all agencies/government branches have active participation, decision-making authority, written mission statement, roles and responsibilities, and liaison point of contacts even if there are not active team member designations. Examples of these collaborations where policies and practices are aligned exist in Maryland, Tennessee, and Arizona among others. All of these examples have worked to streamline procedures and corroborate practices within child serving agencies. For example, Maine established a system for local superintendents to bring together a "reintegration team" ten days prior to a youth's release from a state juvenile facility. In Arizona, the System of Care team developed 12 core principles in working with youth and implemented these principles statewide. California created the Child Welfare Council that oversees practices within all systems serving child welfare youth. Oregon creates partnerships in local communities and state government to align practices of child serving agencies to best fit the unique community. Information on further collaborations can be found at www.forumfyi.org. An additional example of changed sustained by team efforts exists in Pennsylvania, where the county implemented a sharing program between the school system and the Department of Human Services that enables case workers and other child welfare staff to easily access educational records of foster youth. The result of which was the creation of an Education Page in the case workers electronic case record for each child. This served as an added benefit of notification of absences of students electronically (Seigle et al., 2014). All these examples are ways in which the action team created in the county can build collaboration, create change, and sustain improved educational outcomes.

Action Team Barriers

Often, there is tension between various school staff and agency staff for failed previous efforts to plan for a youth's education and all pretenses must be left at the door if collaboration is to succeed. The team must be honest about the systemic barriers, "turf protection," and the differing missions for all of the various agencies/schools involved. Always keep in mind that all professionals are working toward the best interest of youth, they simply have differing views about how to best achieve it. More importantly, any legal barriers that could prevent the effective coordination of services must also be addressed. Action team discussions should be respectful and honest as to what is and is not working within current practices. Make sure not to pin down any particular person at fault within any given agency, but rather work toward describing the broader picture of current policies, practices, and agendas so that any one person or agency is not to blame. Once action team members have a greater understanding of the other, most systemic barriers in educational planning should resolve. Change takes time and systemic changes take even more time.

Each member has valuable feedback in the way in which educational planning can be implemented in the county. As long as discussions are productive, and decisions are made as a result of those discussions, then the action team is moving forward positively. The facilitator can take notes of any issues that are to be discussed at a later time and keep the agenda organized for each meeting. In addition, the existence of different missions within the varying organizations will inevitably arise. All organizations are working with youth in differing capacities and all complement each other in the services provided. As described by Wiig et al. (2013), "it is important to protect the integrity of each system's missions, mandates, and policies but ... a careful examination will help show where the two systems have points in common that serve as a foundation for integration and coordination efforts" (p. 37).

Chapter 8

Creating an Education Action Team

Recruiting Agency Team Members

Action team members are individuals in the agencies and schools who may already be working together in some capacity. Certain agencies are necessary to assemble an effective action team. Often, there is a current collaboration in the county that can be utilized in recruiting potential team members. These collaborations may be targeting other specific areas of need or perhaps be a professional board that oversees general collaborative initiatives. While not all agencies can be active members of the team, all agencies can commit to providing a POC for the action team once it is in place.

It is now time to actively recruit action team members in the community. To this end, consider presenting to a Provider Committee or other interagency collaborations operating in the county. Contact the coordinators of these meetings and request a time to visit and present the vision of creating an Education Action Team. When requesting assistance, consider a tip in electing participants from Leone and Weinberg (2012), "existing interagency relationships can help bring together agency representatives, but strong leadership – along with a willingness to expend resources such as funding and staff time- is crucial to bringing about necessary changes" (p. 43). Assistance will entail each agency representative finding a staff member willing to commit to the mission and be able to facilitate change in their respective agencies with regard to educational planning. Furthermore, it is recommended to also seek representation from the local mental health agency so as to effectively address the specific developmental needs of youth and also address any unique regulations around information sharing. Listed in the key questions table are specific questions agencies can utilize to determine the best point of contact for educational purposes. If contacting agencies via email or mail, create a basic invitation letter or email as a starting point to send to all prospective partners.

For example, the first members of the Douglas County Education Action Team were able to present to the Douglas County 1451 Interagency Oversight Group (IOG) to invite further partners. They were successful in recruiting a representative from additional agencies including all juvenile justice agencies. The IOG serves as an Oversight Board to support implementation within their respective agencies for any procedural changes or training produced by the action team. Within the IOG commitment to the action team, there are several potential partners that can be recruited to participate as more active action team members should the specific need arise. In the 17th Judicial District, the Education Advocate presented the guide concept to the Juvenile Service Provider Committee (JSPC) overseeing the Senate Bill 94 program to gain support toward implementing system procedures that might impact the roles staff play in educational planning.

Below is a comprehensive list of potential partners that can identify an active team member and/or identify a point of contact:

- Child welfare
- Probation
- School Resource Officer (SRO)
- CWEL
- County Attorney
- Public Defenders
- District Attorney's office
- Division of Youth Corrections Representative
- SPED Coordinator
- Court/Judges/Magistrate
- Intervention Services Office in school district
- GAL
- Local mental health agency
- Pre-Trial Supervision agency
- Juvenile Assessment Center
- Diversion

KEY QUESTIONS: AGENCIES

Who are the most responsive and motivated by this cause?

Who engages youth in unique ways?

Who is extremely helpful and passionate about education with clients?

Who is willing to be the point of contact for all education purposes?

Who in your agency is a "boundary spanner," an individual who has knowledge and/or training in two or more child-serving agencies' practices?

Who has a unique understanding of the inner workings of both schools and agencies?

Who has authority to take action and implement change?

Recruiting School Team Members

Recognizing that schools have many different departments and staff interacting with youth on a daily basis, the school district may need to clarify what person and how many people are appointed action team members so as to effectively assist the team not only with streamlining administrative tasks but also with individual school culture which will be discussed in phase 2. For example, Colorado Child Welfare Education Liaisons (CWEL) can be the school district point of contact for outside agencies to assist in all child welfare administrative tasks implemented by the action team such as notification procedures, records transfers, transportation, and best interest determinations. If such a position does not exist in the county, perhaps the homeless liaison is willing to serve as an action team member or a staff within Student Engagement, Student Services, Special Education, Student Intervention Services, or the like. Look toward a school department that is already working with foster care and/or juvenile justice youth in some capacity to supplement the CWEL position and are willing to take on the additional responsibility.

It is often found that the school department that oversees expulsions and discipline has frequent contact with the population and are potentially very strong allies in these efforts. This can be the POC for school culture discussions and efforts to keep and/or re-engage youth in school settings specifically. As a result, teams may have multiple school district representatives and this is encouraged to ensure a more comprehensive picture of the education system and the multiple areas for improvement.

Initial Meeting Considerations

Once the initiator is ready, schedule a date, time, and location to convene the first Education Action Team meeting to then plan for initial focus groups and strategize ways to recruit further members. Some counties may see success with having a judicial staff lead the initiative, but any vested county staff is effective in scheduling and facilitating this first meeting. In Douglas County, meetings began at the courthouse at 12pm so that judges and magistrates can participate, and they have continued to be the same time and location monthly. This timeframe and location are effective in allowing for the participation of many agencies. Initial members from this team included child welfare, magistrates, a CWEL, and a county attorney.

Action Team Logistics

Establish a regular meeting schedule for the first year. This includes location, frequency of meetings, and time frame. Providing food and beverages are often good incentives for active participation and regular attendance. Oftentimes a "working lunch" once a month is a great tool to engage members. It is also helpful to have a judge or magistrate recruit members and engage agencies. Action teams may find that they need to meet more than once a month for the first year. This is often the case but consistent attendance can be difficult. Much of the pre-planning work can be done via email and phone conferencing. Action teams can also write a commitment of a certain percentage of attendance into the agency roles/responsibilities document or the MOU.

Action Team Communications

A solidified action team requires consistent communication strategies to members and to agency staff when implementing changes to improve educational outcomes. A foundation of trust in all members having a commitment to seeing through the actions of change is a must. As mentioned by Wiig et al. (2013), "the key is to be strategic, not secretive" (p. 13). A leader must be selected to facilitate meetings and partner with consultants to keep communications moving forward productively. If there is not a consultant or meeting facilitator, select a team member to take meeting minutes and a team member to maintain the contact/distribution list so all parties are informed of current events within the team. Within their respective agencies/schools, the members must decide how they will train and spread information with new procedural changes to staff as well.

Chapter 9

Action Team

Initial Agenda

Focus Groups

When designing the action team, it is important to have a clear picture of county needs, gaps in communication, and procedural breakdowns specifically regarding educational stability. When convening the action team, it is important to document these specific concerns to guide action team agenda items and specific goals, mission, and values. It also helps to establish the collaborative effort of all agencies and the school district when each member discovers the current roles/responsibilities of all other agencies at the table. This action will prompt the initial discussion of any existent communication barriers or misunderstandings about roles. This focus group session will also help to establish a baseline for collecting data. With an initial list of all the gaps in service, the team can measure, in a designated time after implementation, how much those concerns were addressed. It offers a way to gauge effectiveness of the team as well as monitor implementation of procedures in each agency. Listed below are questions the facilitator can ask and document from the focus group. The focus group discussion should happen within the first few meetings of the action team while conversations of the MOU and identifying points of contact are also on the agenda. This focus group might take up anywhere from one to three meetings. The length of time it takes to identify problem areas is entirely individual to each county. It is important to have a moderator who is neutral and not a part of the action team.

KEY QUESTIONS: FOCUS GROUPS

What are you biggest gaps in services?

Where are all children falling "through the cracks" educationally?

What collaborations already exist?

Examples of when transitions have gone well? What role did your agency play?

Are there examples of school staff collaboration with outside agencies?

Existing protocol for sharing/sending educational records for court-involved youth?

Are these transfers timely, effective, and where are the gaps in service?

What is the current MOU for educational planning?

Who are the current points of contact within agencies and schools?

What agency keeps a youth's educational file other than school?

What educational planning systems are in place for juvenile justice youth?

What are the differences between juvenile justice youth and child welfare youth educational planning?

Is the Crossover Youth Model implemented in the county?

What are the most utilized day and residential treatment centers?

Action Team MOU

In order to ensure that all members are committed to the team and the work that may be required, it is helpful to create an MOU. Within this document be sure to consider all aspects that can be included as the literature suggests that "agencies can formalize expectations related to these meetings and other collaborative activities through memorandums of understanding that specify parties' roles and responsibilities; written interagency protocols and policy and procedure manuals, and blended funding initiatives that combine resources from multiple systems to support shared processes and services" (Seigle et al., 2014, p. 71). At minimum for the purposes of this action team, this MOU should state the mission of the team, roles/responsibilities that pertain to committing as a team member and outline an agreement for information sharing of individual youth.

Information sharing will assist not only in the timeliness of individual educational planning but also in data collection for showing effectiveness. It allows for the ability to track educational outcomes of youth long term. However, there is the chance a county may find that a MOU is no longer necessary if all information sharing is in place and the proper release forms are utilized across all agencies. When making this decision, ensure the action team is still able to track outcome data without the MOU or any additional information sharing barriers. Action team members can review what releases are being utilized and decide what will best suit the needs of the team moving forward so as to prevent any barriers to information sharing. As mentioned by Gonsoulin et al. (2012), all systems, "should adopt and embrace a culture of openness and willingness to share academic, behavioral, and other relevant information among staff, mental health and medical professionals, security personnel and other discipline-related staff, case managers, and any others playing an active role in the education and care of a youth involved with the juvenile or child welfare system" (p. 6). The action team absolutely must address any barriers for information sharing not only within the action team but for all individual cases when discussing this option. If the MOU is necessary, be sure to include information sharing responsibilities of team members to share outcome data. If releases need to be revised, many Colorado agencies now utilize the state HIPPAA release form that is available online: https://cdpsdocs.state.co.us/oajja/ccyis/StateofColoradoAuthorizationConsentto ReleaseInformation9_26_13.pdf

Mission Statement Guidelines

The next step in initial establishment of the action team is to create a mission statement under which all work will fall. This statement should encompass the overall purpose of the action team. A general guideline reads, "The action team is working towards (X), to accomplish (Y) with the overall purpose of effecting (Z)."

In Douglas County, the mission statement reads: *To improve and establish the processes that reduce or eliminate the barriers to school success faced by children and families within the child welfare and/or juvenile justice system in Douglas County.*

Action Team Member Responsibilities

It is important to clearly define the responsibilities of all agencies with regard to educational planning, not only at a systems level but individual level as well. Each agency has a unique contribution and approach to working with youth. Agencies will also have differing levels of access to information including courts, child welfare, juvenile records, and general/special education records. Representatives will have varying levels of involvement in a case and some will enter into a case at a different time from the initial youth point of entry. Accordingly, their contribution to the action team will be three-fold. First, they commit as the POC to the team for outside agencies as an initial contact for educational planning. Second, there is the role that their agency staff serves in individual education planning and outlining that to the action team so as to further enhance that role. Finally, there is the role of disseminating the information to their respective agencies in regard to new educational planning procedures. This includes assisting in the coordinating any cross-agency training. This member commitment lays the groundwork to achieve what the research recommends in providing juvenile education by formalizing and standardizing policies and procedures, allowing for consistent education services across all systems serving youth (National Juvenile Justice Network, 2016).

Throughout the recommendations by national child welfare and juvenile justice agencies, it is clear that establishing interagency protocols to share information on youth status and designating specific liaisons within each agency to implement these protocols can help all systems work together seamlessly. Establishing the POC role allows for streamlining initial agency contact for education purposes. For example, the relevant Juvenile Probation Unit appointed a Juvenile Team Supervisor as a member of the Douglas County Education Action Team. As that point of contact, any caseworker, therapist, school staff, and so on can contact this person and request assistance in locating the proper probation officer for a particular youth.

Each representative should draft a team member role description based on the agency in which he/she works. This description includes a commitment to serve as the POC both in and outside of their agency and the description of how their agency staff is involved in the educational planning process specifically. This document is then signed by that agency representative, solidifying the commitment to the team for the first year. Another option to receive commitment from members is to consider including these roles/responsibilities with the MOU agreement for information sharing.

Action Team Member Role Definitions

To assist with writing this document, below are the potential roles each POC can play on the action team within their agencies. Agency team members can take an active role in creating a paradigm shift on the equal importance of education in their agency. It is important to understand the fundamental aspects of what agencies are already doing with youth and what the potential is for growth in that role with regard to educational planning.

Child Welfare: As an action team member, the POC can provide an overview of the process of child welfare involvement and where education planning can be initiated. It is then a joint effort of the action team to explore the details of those procedures. Caseworkers are often the keepers of the educational files for youth; however, they often do not have the necessary time to facilitate in-depth educational planning to ensure all academic needs are met. In order for caseworkers to be successful in educational planning, the action team POC will need to clarify the role a caseworker has in educational planning. Also keep in mind that caseworkers will have different levels of contact with youth at certain times in the system and the agency POC can work through those specifics with the action team. The POC for child welfare should be a supervisor, program manager, director, or the like who can help implement new educational planning protocol in the most streamlined and effective way for all caseworkers specific to the department in which they work. This process ensures that regardless of what child welfare department has the case, educational need is prioritized.

Probation: As an action team member, the POC can provide an overview of the judicial system and the post-adjudication processes. They can also speak to how a youth can be "out of compliance" with probation in relation to education expectations and what consequences may ensue as a result. Individual officers develop relationships with juveniles and can also promote school attendance and accountability and that might be beneficial for the action team to build upon when creating educational planning roles for probation officers.

School Resource Officer (SRO): The role of an SRO can vary greatly from school to school in terms of how interactive they are with individual students. It is helpful for an SRO agency team member to provide information on their potential role and how they wish to help. SROs can possibly help identify truant students and make home visits. SROs often have the ability to build positive relationships with students and foster a sense of community on campus. SROs can take an interest and build positive relationships with foster and juvenile justice youth, thus taking on a role of positive adult mentor.

CWEL: The position is designed to be the school POC for any foster or juvenile youth but the role will look different in each school district. The action team CWEL should take time to speak about how their role has evolved and what potential it has for growth. The action team should work with CWEL to gauge the level of availability in terms of implementing procedural change, providing direct service of youth, and potentially monitoring progress of identified youth. In this framework, the CWEL is the POC for all educational information when a youth enters into the system and connects agencies with appropriate school staff.

County Attorney: The County Attorney can assist the action team in explaining the legalities of child welfare. They can work through the child welfare process with the action team in discovering ways in which they can assist in the paradigm shift of education importance at the court level. On an individual level, County Attorneys can be helpful in the appointment of ESP or CASA for educational signing rights.

Public Defenders: Public Defenders should take the time to explain where they can potentially assist in promoting education while a youth is in pre-adjudication proceedings. It is helpful to know how much interest the Public Defenders have taken in education up until this point and how much they can contribute moving forward. In Colorado, the Public Defender's office now employs social workers and this has the potential for a partnership with the action team. That social worker can be a POC and may be willing to assist in arranging training PDs on varying topics such as adolescent development, general or special education needs, trauma informed care, and so on.

District Attorney's Office: The DA's office is responsible for notifying schools on new charges of a youth in the school. The team can revisit this notification form as it related to action team goals, plans, and any relevant information that can be added to enhance this form.

Division of Youth Services (DYS) Representative: Corrections workers and parole officers are primarily responsible for transitions out of facilities after a commitment to corrections. This action team member can explain exactly how that transition is taking place currently and its effectiveness when the team begins to explore how other transitions take place so as to determine how all education transitions will evolve. This will allow for education transitions to look similar for every youth each time throughout the continuum of services. Training can be coordinated for DYS staff on county specific policies and procedures in education transition so as to improve the process and keep it consistent across all systems. This representative can also be utilized as the POC on newly committed youth for an ES who worked with the youth to ensure all pre-commitment educational records are received by the new facility.

Special Education (SPED) Coordinator: These professionals can assist in incorporating the unique dynamics of foster and juvenile justice youth when working with special education youth. Additionally, they can cultivate awareness about the needs of this population and foster creativity in how to incorporate these needs into special education goals within IEP. They can attend training and take new information back to direct service special education staff such as teachers and case managers. This contact could also be willing to train outside agencies on SPED or develop a special education handout for professionals. In some cases the CWEL may be the Out of District SPED Coordinator.

Court Coordinator or Judge/Magistrate: This person often can be the director of the action team efforts. They can support training of court staff and ensure that procedures and best practices are being implemented by other staff while reviewing cases in court. Judges/magistrates often see the overall bigger picture of the gaps in service as a case unfolds in the courtroom with all parties present. Judges and magistrates should take time to explain their unique position and how they envision their role to further promote educational stability.

School District Intervention Services Office: This position can coordinate discipline and safety measures in schools for juveniles. This person also promotes best practice for keeping youth in school verses defaulting to out of school suspensions or expulsions as the consequence for all discipline matters. This is a crucial member of the action team to assist with enhancing individual work with youth in schools.

Guardian Ad Litem (GAL): This position can act as an Educational Surrogate Parent (ESP) and take an active role in the educational planning and meetings of youth. However, because all GALs operate within their own agency, their involvement cases varies depending on their availability, priorities, and case load. GALs are invited to participate in setting school progress meetings and any discipline measures such as expulsion hearings but do not always do so. GAL POC can share information on action team efforts to other GALs working in the county to also encourage them to take an active role in educational planning. The GAL POC should work to achieve consistency in the expectation of the position specific to educational planning so other agencies are able to trust a GAL to fulfill certain duties.

Local Mental Health Agency: The local mental health agency can present to the action team as to how clients can best access their support and get enrolled for services. They can explain all the access points for mental health supports in the various agencies and schools so as not to duplicate services. The mental health POC can provide training to staff on mental health agency practices and also how mental health most directly effects youth in the classroom. Mental health agencies can assist the action team in removing any identified barriers in information sharing with schools about a youth's mental health, so school staff are more appropriately informed of mental health impact in the classroom.

Juvenile Assessment Center (JAC): This is typically the first contact of juvenile youth and can initiate education stability in the forefront of a case. The JAC POC can explain, to the action team, the purpose of the assessment center, clarify assessments utilized, and review the screening process. More importantly, the JAC POC can work with the action team to create specific education intake questions to determine the level of a youth's education needs. They can then relay that information to court staff, attorneys, pre-trial, probation, residential treatment, and/or child welfare. JAC also has the ability to notify the school district of the JAC visit and the outcome of a visit, whether criminal justice or voluntary status to prompt school collaboration.

Pre-Trial Supervision Agency: After the assessment center, the pre-trial supervision agency often supervises a youth in the community while awaiting sentencing on new charges. The POC for the action team can explain all the expectations and services available to the youth while under pre-trial supervision. This will be especially helpful to school staff and child welfare staff who may not know the difference between pre-trial and probation supervision. This agency can then work with the action team to implement educational intake questions with the youth to immediately determine the level of educational services needed.

Diversion: Diversion POC can explain the level of offenders under their supervision and what educational planning they are already doing in their own offices as they are often separate from both pre-trial and probation. Diversion has the opportunity to work in coordination with these agencies via the action team so all are coordinating with schools in a similar manner. Diversion officers are in a unique role where they can take an active role in connecting first time offenders with educational supports as a *preventative* measure against any further system involvement.

Identifying Data and Statistics

In order to have effective data collection to report effectiveness on the Education Action Team, teams must first establish a baseline of data that is available in the county. Review the data available for mobility rates, crossover youth, foster care youth graduation rates, and juvenile justice recidivism rates. Also, compare the state foster care youth data available through Colorado Department of Education with county-specific outcomes. To this end, the data collection will also relate to gaps in service identified in the focus group as to what data is not currently collected. This will help the team determine what data should be collected during this process and if a new simple database needs development specific to track all educational services and new process effectiveness.

Data Collection

Within the action team, determine who will collect the data throughout the implementation of systems change. This may be the individuals directly impacted by systems change such as the CWEL, education direct service staff, or employees/team members committed to the cause. The action team might also want to consider bringing in an outside evaluation firm to best collect all data possible in the efforts to show effectiveness. This is particularly important if the action team is attempting to show the need for funding of specific educational services positions. Consider all forms of data collection to ensure a comprehensive view of impacted systems such as pre and post surveys, questionnaires, interviews, focus groups of youth and families, review of case files, and any further forms of data collection the team deems beneficial (Brock et al., 2008).

In both the 17th Judicial District and Douglas County, a simple excel database was developed for the tracking of specific numbers the team sought to improve. The Douglas County CWEL maintains a database of notifications received as well as the Educational Navigator creating a simple database to track the number of youth provided direct service as well as the type of service received. In addition, the Adams County school district CWELs maintain a simple database to track school district specific notifications of juvenile justice youth by listing name, school, special education status, discipline, and if educational services are provided. This data can be used to track educational outcomes at a later time. More importantly, counties may want to consider tracking educational attainment as it relates to recidivism as this is a crucial positive result this framework can impact. Each fiscal year, teams should work with the juvenile justice POC to track youth who receive educational specific services against those who do not and compare recidivism rates for each. Also, school can report educational attainment for juvenile justice youth to determine if recidivism rates were lower for those with educational attainment. Educational attainment is classified as passing classes in a school term, advancing a grade level, and/or graduation.

The team may need to consider a specific written agreement in which entities commit to tracking data and measuring outcomes of the team efforts if this was not already done in the MOU as previously mentioned. This was the case in the 17th Judicial District where an information sharing agreement is in place, ensuring that school district POC assumed responsibilities to collect data on youth for which they receive juvenile justice notifications. This agreement outlines how the juvenile justice information will be used and shared within the individual schools to provide positive support to youth. One must always consider how the additional workload of data collection impacts current workload of individuals. It is important to separate information collected on youth who receive educational services versus those who do not so as to measure effectiveness of work. If the team establishes a point of data collection and there is a change in direction for any reason, the team will need to revisit the target measures.

KEY QUESTIONS: DATA COLLECTION

What agencies have what information related to education outcomes?

What data and current stats are available by which to measure improvements and success?

What data does team deem most important and relevant to goals?

What, if any, positive outcomes are tracked?

For example, in Douglas County, the team prioritized the creation of procedures for Best Interest Determinations when a youth is removed from the home and placed in foster care. At first, the team set the intention to review each case in the past year and collect data on length of time youth spent awaiting enrollment in a new school after out of home removal. However, this proved difficult given the full-time job responsibilities of each team member. Instead, the team utilized existent data showing that out of 266 students removed from care the previous year, the CWEL received notification on only 7 of these cases. With this baseline data collected, the team created and implemented Best Interest Determination procedures to ensure consistent notification to the CWEL every time a youth was removed from the home. At the end of the first year, the team will collect data again on the youth removed from the home to compare how many notifications the CWEL received from the previous year. This then allows for a review in process to adjust procedures and further identify continued service gaps. This data collection assists in the action team creating second year goals as well.

In the 17th Judicial District, the Education Advocate compares recidivism rates for those youth receiving direct educational planning successfully each year. The program is also able to track successful follow-up information if the youth is still enrolled following a closure date for up to three months consistently and potentially six months if within the one-year signed release. For example, in FY 2014–2015, the Education Advocate maintained a 72% success rate upon closing education services. At a one-month follow-up, 93% were still enrolled and attending. At a three-month follow-up, 87% were still enrolled and attending. Ideally, the action team should track educational attainment, enrollment, and attendance long-term through graduation if possible. Consider drawing a small sample of youth to track long-term in this way to further identify patterns of what educational service is most utilized and useful.

Examples of Effectiveness Measurements

Below is a list of examples that action teams can utilize as a way to show effectiveness. This will also depend on what baseline data is available.

Increase attendance.
Increase in core (math and reading) academic grades per semester.
Number of days enrolled in schools.
Increase number of individual student education plans created at school with youth team.
Increase number of transition plans for court-involved youth.
Increase rate of educational intakes of youth.
Decreased wait time for foster care youth in new school enrollment.
Increase youth staying in home school despite being removed from home.
Increase amount of best interest determinations with every home placement.
Decrease the amount of school transitions for a youth in the child welfare system.
Increase proficiency in core areas of math and reading.

Did student remain in school or dropout within 30, 60, 90 days following closure of case?

Decrease recidivism rates for students who received direct educational service planning.

Did student decide to pursue a diploma or a GED?

Number of days it took for a youth in special education to receive an IEP meeting upon entry into school.

In addition to measuring client data, the process of systemic changes can be well documented by surveying perception of improvements by staff working in the field. It is recommended that the action team create an initial survey for team members and agency staff to measure the perceptions of educational planning effectiveness at the start of the team and at the end of the first year to measure perceived improvements. This is also a chance for staff to provide feedback about possible improvements to new system procedures to further improve service delivery.

When taking this step in what measures will be utilized, please know that data collection in showing effectiveness is an intricate process far beyond keeping a simple database of client data and one initial focus group. Data collection can span well beyond what has been done so far in both Douglas and the 17th Judicial District. This is partly due to the lack of need to prove effectiveness for funding measures. Both the 17th JD Education Advocate and the Educational Navigator were positions that were implemented by adjusting the respective budgets of those agencies. There are important aspects in creating all types of data collection, including how to phrase survey questions, outcome evaluation methods, and the environment in which data is collected from the audience. Consider utilizing both quantitative and qualitative data collection methods to show effectiveness so the action team can provide feedback both by a numeric value and personal perspectives of those impacted by procedural changes. An example of quantitative data includes surveys and evaluations with Likert scale ratings, while qualitative data is collected by focus groups or other personal interactions. Those impacted includes both professionals and clients. As mentioned above, an outside moderator, consultant, or research group is ideal for rigorous evaluation measures.

Action Plan Goals and Objectives

The team is designed to *produce* change not simply to *discuss* change. The team is comprised of individuals who have a passion for improving educational outcomes and it may feel as though it is a "grassroots" effort. Action team members are individuals that have a working knowledge of direct service along with the ability to identify exactly where the systemic gaps exist throughout the child welfare and juvenile justice process during initial focus groups. These individuals can also identify what processes are realistic for implementation at the direct service level. As a result, utilize focus group outcomes first and foremost to establish an action plan.

Utilizing the focus group answers, the action team can now identify three main goals for the team over the next year and draft an initial action plan. Goals are centered on the vision of ensuring that educational planning is on the forefront of every case and starts the moment a youth comes into the court system via child welfare or juvenile justice. Each agency has feedback about points of entry and their own intake procedures for when a youth comes into the system. This framework is not a temporary fix and will take increased coordination of systems to implement for long-term sustainability. To that end, the goals established will promote the permanent paradigm shift toward the importance of educational planning in every case every time. Goals should promote education planning as important as all other areas of service throughout the entire length of the case, from open to close.

While finalizing goals and writing the action plan, ensure that overall goals will specifically show a marked improvement in the education planning of court-involved youth. Listed below are some key goals and objectives that, if implemented, will assist in improving educational outcomes. In addition, a sample action plan document is included for use in the Appendix.

KEY GOALS AND OBJECTIVES

Develop flow chart of procedures for educational planning of court-involved youth.

Develop and sustain professional development and cross-agency training plan.

Establish, train, and implement a School District Notification document for child welfare Involvement.

Establish, train, and implement a School District Notification document for Juvenile Justice Involvement.

Establish Best Interest Determinations procedures and protocol.

Establish point of contact procedures for educational planning.

Establish educational planning procedures across systems upon entry into the juvenile justice system.

Establish education transitions procedures consistent for all education transitions across systems.

Establish a day reporting program for unenrolled youth to re-engage in education.

Develop a specific educational intake procedure and document for use in the field.

Adapt and implement this Guide's CWEL policy and procedures.

Adapt and implement interventions in phase 3 of this framework.

Partner with the school district to keep youth continuously enrolled despite any child welfare or juvenile justice involvement.

Chapter 10

Action Team in Action

Creating and Establishing New Procedures

The system changes advised in this guide are not changing the entire system protocol; it is simply evaluating the current procedures for educational planning and streamlining the process. In the end, direct service workers are required to do the same amount or perhaps less work than before. Through the discussions of the gaps in service and current protocols, teams will find that there are duplications in current education planning and these will be streamlined by developing and implementing new procedures.

Once the team has formalized visual diagrams and finalized new processes as related to action plan goals, the action team will work on training staff on the new process. Next, while in the implementation phase, iron out any kinks in the process, identify continued service gaps, check for weaknesses in the system, and revise any new forms. Create a brief PowerPoint as a basic training instruction on new process. Team members must work together in creating a training resource for all agency staff on any new procedures within all the different agencies. It is important to provide visual and written documentation of all new procedures. Ideally, if there is an ES, this person can organize and facilitate the training. As with any new procedure, full implementation will take time. Repeated training and consistency is required by the ES or action team POC within their respective agencies and they will need to remind staff regularly about new procedures until full implementation occurs. Keep in mind the action team should be utilized to problem solve any flaws in the new system and modify as deemed necessary. Be sure that this new procedure becomes a standard in new employee manuals and training so as to establish a clear sustained change in service delivery.

Tips from the Field

Listed below are programs that are available in other states that were established through collaboration efforts.

- Project U Turn in Philly (www.projectuturn.net/ System). Offers opportunities for students on the basis of their age, literacy and numeracy levels, and credits earned. Project U Turn developed the E3 program for juvenile and out of school youth to re-engage.
- Crossover Youth Model designed by Georgetown University and implemented nationally (http://cjjr.georgetown.edu/our-work/crossover-youth-practice-model/).

- Nevada Task Force (www.ktvn.com/story/33821360/ nevada-task-force-considers-improvements- to-juvenile-justice-system).
- Palm Beach County, Florida: Second Chance Act Reentry Taskforce. When a youth in the child welfare system is arrested, the juvenile intake worker immediately notifies the child welfare social worker and both parties conduct a joint case review initially and continue to collaborate on the case until it is closed (www.pbcgov.com/criminaljustice/).
- Washington State Education Advocacy Program Manual (www.k12.wa.us/InstitutionalEd/WashingtonsEducationAdvocate.aspx).
- Academic and Career/Technical Training Alliance (PACTT) in Pennsylvania is an example of an action team direct service assigned to ensure that youth in correctional facilities receive rigorous, relevant, and high-quality education and vocational training. The PACTT staff liaisons coordinate services within all agencies (www.pactt-alliance.org/Pages/default.aspx).

Phase 2

Systems Interventions

Chapter 11

Phase 2 Introduction

Phase 2 is a construct for connecting juvenile justice systems with schools. It walks through processes for defining existing positions, improving and revising systems procedures, creating cross-agency training, and fostering opportunities to initiate conversations about school accommodation for this youth population. Coordinating systems in phase 2 is possible as a direct result of the action team and collaboration established in phase 1. With the action team in place, agencies can evaluate the current county procedures and identify fundamental points of entry where educational planning will be inserted. Phase 2 focuses on the top opportunities to directly impact outcomes and systems change, but the team is certainly not limited to these specific improvements.

The first part of phase 2 is identifying current county procedures and determining how school notification procedures will be implemented. The process in which systems notify schools must be defined and implemented in order to set educational planning roles and procedural shifts in motion. Notification procedures implemented by the action team will determine how the CWEL position is utilized and how education transition procedures are improved.

The second part of phase 2 discusses specific procedural changes, highlighting how systems can create improvements and/or new processes. Though other procedures can be the central focus for initiating change, best interest determinations (BIDs) and education transition procedures are the examples that will be used to outline systematic coordination among schools, agencies, and families. These procedures require multi-system coordination and are targeted here because the coordination may not be seamless for some counties, which presents a need for closing gaps in services and formalizing processes. Next, phase 2 covers procedures relevant toward education transition amidst the numerous transitions youth face in both child welfare and juvenile justice from shorter detention stays to longer residential facility stays.

This phase can indirectly impact current disciplinary procedures on youth. According to Seigle et al. (2014), Colorado requires the principal of each school to submit an annual written report to the district board of education regarding the school's learning environment. The report includes totals for conduct and discipline code violations that include weapon possession, drug possession, disobedience, and disturbing the learning environment. Since many of the court-involved youth contribute to these totals, it behooves schools and agencies to partner on methods to reduce incidence of such youth behaviors and, hopefully, decrease the number of discipline code violations in the school. This part of phase 2 also contributes to the possibility of lowering juvenile justice totals—criminal justice involvement and recidivism are less likely when youth are continuously enrolled in school.

This is a key piece to keeping youth successful in school despite negative and detrimental behaviors that disrupt the school environment. This youth population needs multiple chances to get back on track. When schools push youth out due to a discipline issue following a transition, it decreases momentum and increases the chance of school failure. As each agency is working to update procedures to establish education as a crucial element of case planning, the school also plays a role in working with agencies to keep youth in school once enrolled and this might mean creating a paradigm shift in how a school views these youth. In other words, by considering juvenile justice-involved youth as more than a criminal and meeting them with more compassion and understanding, there is an opportunity to change the dynamic in interactions between school staff and youth on a daily basis. There are reasons that youth act out and the youth population involved in the justice system may have experienced trauma and negative events that are better addressed through compassion from caring adults instead of discipline. Outside agencies have the expertise and capacity to train school staff and offer tactics that will help shift cultural views of these youth to change negative interaction, further emphasizing the need for true collaboration among schools and systems. Schools must be willing to explore options that will allow juvenile justice-involved youth to return to school safely and effectively, even if that means allowing youth to *try again and again and again*. As previously noted, a juvenile justice record does not define future potential, so it is incumbent for systems to operate from that fundamental belief every single time. What works for 90% of the general education population may not work for court-involved youth for the numerous reasons already discussed. The important piece is to show a vested interest in the youth and adopt a *we will not give up on you* attitude particularly if they are still attempting to re-connect with school community. Some youth may have never experienced this type of support in their families and will need it from school staff up through graduation.

It should be noted that a major school district discipline reform is not required for this framework to be effective. The purpose of the guide is to offer a realistic and manageable method for the action team to impart change in individual schools within a flawed system. However, do not be held back by this guide. If a school district is in pursuit of a large-scale school discipline reform, it is still to the advantage of youth for the action team to collaborate and partner in those efforts.

Finally, the importance of cross-agency training is in developing a shared understanding of various roles and systems involved in direct services, including underlying principles held by the agencies, youth, and their families. Initial and ongoing training across agencies eliminates confusion about roles and responsibilities. This guide includes both cross agency and formal professional training for all agencies, schools, and families, as systems and schools benefit from a basic understanding of general policies and procedures at play. This is particularly true if it is necessary to implement new educational procedures; all systems need to understand their specific role in each procedure. One of the goals in this guide is to avoid creating additional barriers for youth caused by professionals' lack of cross-system knowledge. Action teams may find that stakeholder agencies know each other's roles very well in a general sense, but they lack the tactical knowledge that enables efficient actions in educational planning—a typical example is having shared understanding that a school needs to be contacted, but there is not agreement about who should be contacted and when. The guide provides steps for identifying training needs between agency and school, as well as agency to agency.

Phase 2 Key Terms

Notification of Child Welfare or Juvenile Justice Involvement Form: The notification form initiates educational planning when youth are involved in child welfare or juvenile justice, and it is the first procedural step implemented by the action team. A sample notification form is provided in the Appendix for adaptation. If this step is not in place and/or no other form of notification is in place, revisit with the action team before moving forward.

Education Direct Service Staff or ES: Any education staff providing individual direct educational planning for youth is known herein as "ES." The ES could be an educational advocate, coordinator, navigator, liaison, or similar staff.

Home school district and receiving school district: The home school district is the school district in which the youth resides prior to being involved with child welfare/child welfare or juvenile justice. The receiving school district is the new school district in which youth is enrolling.

Cross-agency training: This is the training that members of the action team will develop to introduce their respective agencies/schools to other agencies while also introducing new procedures. Cross-agency training needs to be sustainable and conducted yearly.

Best Interest Determination (BID): A BID is a mandated discussion regarding school placement when youth are removed from the home, both for emergent and non-emergent removals. BIDs must be completed within a defined timeframe to determine whether youth shall remain in the home school with transportation provided or move to a new school of placement.

Education Transition Planning: The practice of planning around youth transitions, including transitions into or out of residential placement, districts, and/or community schools. Effective education transition planning considers the unique circumstances for each individual, the transition, and other areas of need. Other areas of need often include but are not limited to mental health, education, family services, therapeutic services, substance abuse outpatient services, employment, mentorship, and connections to community resources. Education transition is a specific area of need that should be included consistently in an overall transition plan.

Transition Summary: The Transition Summary is a document utilized in the field and seeks the most valuable information for the receiving school in preparation for enrollment. This document was adopted by the 17th JD Education Advocate after reviewing existing transition documents already utilized in the field. The sample in the Appendix can be used by the action team in a similar way to create a transition document that is relevant to the county in which it is implemented.

Child Welfare Education Liaison (CWEL): The school district is required to appoint a point of contact for all foster care youth for immediate assistance with enrollment. This position is known as the Child Welfare Education Liaison or CWEL in Colorado. A list is maintained on the Colorado Department of Education website identifying the CWELs in every school district. Other states may have a court-involved youth contact by a different name. If this position does not exist, make it a goal of the action team to establish that point of contact.

Special Education (SPED): When general education is impeded due to a disability, special education services help with learning and education accessibility for youth who qualify. These accommodations, service hours, and goals are documented on an Individual Education Plan (IEP) and are reviewed annually during annual IEP staffing. Youth are tested every three years (Triennial Review) to reassess the need for continued special education eligibility.

Chapter 12

Coordination of Systems to Schools

Review of Current County Procedures

Specifically, within current methods, small steps of educational planning will be woven in/out of the child welfare and juvenile justice process. To determine where this will occur, the action team must clearly outline every step of the child welfare and juvenile justice system. This process will help with every key goal and objective identified by the team in phase I. It is a necessary piece of improving educational outcomes and placing educational planning at the forefront of every case. It is helpful to map out the current process of a case in the form of a flow chart. This flow chart should reflect the time a youth enters and exits the system, including each agency that became involved and when the various points of involvement occurs. This process will map out a clear understanding of the most crucial process points within the current systems and determine what reforms are possible. Once the team has a visual diagram of current systems, they can begin to discuss where the breakdown in communication on educational planning is occurring and where possible points of entry for planning exist. This is the phase where the team will have productive action-oriented discussions on potential system procedural improvements and begin to formulate a plan for implementation. An example of an effective first step in systems change is to establish a procedure of notifying school districts of systems involvement. Once notification is established, the action team can identify responsibilities of staff when the notification is received. Below is an overview of notification processes both from child welfare and juvenile justice. This notification process also serves as a preventative approach as well as identifying youth to the school as youth whose academic progress should be monitored and supported due to systems involvement and risk of decline. As a result of notification procedures, the CWEL position will need definition and a specific flow chart as to what a school CWEL does once notification is received; therefore, sample procedures for that position are described as well.

School District Notification: Child Welfare

Once the team has developed a flow chart on the current child welfare intake process, the decision of how to best notify school district of child welfare involvement must be addressed. Utilize this flow chart in determining what child welfare department and staff will have this responsibility. In previous years, a "School District Notification of Removal" form was implemented within Colorado. However, this notification was only utilized to notify a school district that a child was placed in residential care and was in need of special education service costs. This form may or may not be helpful to the action team now but is worth mentioning if it is working effectively in the county. In other states, identify the current notifications that a school district receives in all realms from all agencies of child welfare involvement. Moreover, identify what the school district staff does once notification is received. As a county, there are various ways in which a school district and/or an ES becomes involved for educational planning purposes and it is possible that adjusting processes around the current notification form might be the way to initiate school district involvement. Next, review current procedures and decide if any are worth formalizing or if it is necessary to adopt new procedures to consistently notify schools and trigger all educational planning.

This is a helpful first step in improving educational outcomes in any county. Simply notifying a school that a youth is court-involved triggers more awareness and support. To be most effective, the team must establish the way in which school districts are notified of both child welfare and juvenile justice involvement at the time of youth systems entry consistently, with every single youth every single time, no exceptions. If the action team does not establish this process, the contents of this guide will not work as well as intended. This process of notification may take time to fully implement but it is an extremely effective way to begin streamlining educational planning procedures.

School District Notification: Juvenile Justice

In each Judicial District in Colorado, the District Attorney (DA) is required to provide written notice to the home school district when youth have obtained criminal charges. It is up to the school district to decide what is done with this information, if anything. In addition, the DA does not list further contact information such as the supervising agency information. For other states, this may look different and certainly the POC for juvenile justice agencies can speak to current notification procedures. To begin, the action team should review the current notification process and create a flow chart of services beginning at point of entry into the juvenile justice system. This will be specific to each Judicial District based on how effective the current process is and how the notification form is utilized in the school district. It is possible that the DA can revise the notification letter to include a POC for further information. On another note, perhaps the action team can establish an ES position that receives immediate notifications and can inform home school district CWEL prompting them to gather records and review academic standing. Whatever the process becomes, be sure to give the school district enough information to prompt building a foundation of support around youth in the current academic community. If the school district does not have enough information, they are left to their own devices to assume the worst and initiate processes to keep other students safe in the school. This may mean a threat assessment, unnecessary behavior or safety plans, strict ISMP's without agency input or indirect targeting of a "bad" youth.

For example, in the 17th Judicial District, the decision was made to send notification of involvement from the local juvenile assessment center. For many at-risk youth, this is the initial point of entry in both voluntary cases seeking assistance and involuntary criminal charge cases. The new protocol includes instructions for the juvenile assessment center staff to inform youth and family about school district notification and its purpose during the intake process. This also provides an opportunity for a guardian or youth to ask for educational assistance. An intake and screen includes collecting history from the youth and the parent and providing recommendations for services. For involuntary intake, or juvenile arrests, screens also include a Colorado Juvenile Risk Assessment to determine risk to the community, which influences placement in either detention or home. The notification includes name, date of birth, placement as a result of screen, contact information for parent and/or agencies involved, and service recommendations. To fully define this process, the Adams County juvenile justice educational services flow chart was designed in partnership with the local school district CWELs, and it highlights the various outcomes for youth once screening is completed via the juvenile assessment center. In all outcomes, school district CWEL is notified of the youth and a step-by-step process in each scenario is clearly displayed. Adams County has eight school districts and the 17th Judicial District includes two additional school districts. To clarify school district contacts for the juvenile assessment center, the 17th Judicial District Education Advocate maintains an up to date contact list for the multiple school districts. Once family/youth identifies school of origin, the juvenile assessment center staff refers to a school contact list, identifies the district CWEL for that particular school, and emails the CWEL notification of juvenile justice involvement.

To solidify this collaboration, an information sharing agreement is in place to ensure the information utilized for collaborative educational planning and not as a means to "target" youth due to juvenile justice involvement. The agreement also mandates that school districts track the notifications and school services in an excel database. As time goes on and procedures begin to run more smoothly, the juvenile assessment center may make adjustments or insert new procedures into the procedural manual. Such updates will be tailored to add clarity about how to speak with families and individuals about school district notification, documentation, and what support to expect from school districts as a result, so all incoming staff are informed as well. This description of school partnership is meant to establish a positive paradigm shift of transparency and support rather than the outdated assumption that a school will use information against youth. A formal process still occurs once the DA files the charges in court in the form of a DA notification letter and is not impacted by this new process. A sample notification form is in the Appendix.

Points of Contact Utilization

As directed in phase 1, the action team has identified POC for every agency working with youth and maintains a contact list of these individuals which can be utilized in phase 2. Within each of these systems is the potential for many different people working in different capacities to directly affect a youth. For example, there may be a school-based therapist, social worker, counselor, dean, special education case manager, registrar, and/or safety service provider interacting with youth on a regular basis. Moreover, a youth can have multiple caseworkers and officers while moving through the child welfare and juvenile justice systems. Efforts to streamline this process include a POC for each of the three largest systems where multiple staff have contact with youth (child welfare, juvenile justice, and school district) and are interfacing with each other on individual cases regularly. Once a youth enters the child welfare system or juvenile justice system, the agency involved at the point of entry can refer to the action team's POC contact list and initiate educational planning that involves all agencies and the school within one email. Each POC can connect the agency professional and individual school staff working directly with the youth thus further triggering the creation of a youth team. If the notification of involvement was automatically sent to the school, they will know that the youth is involved and can connect professionals quickly. This POC utilization further streamlines the process of initiating educational planning upon systems entry.

Chapter 13

Child Welfare Education Liaison Role Description and Procedures

As a result of establishing school district notification and utilizing the CWEL in this process, the CWEL needs to identify what next steps are necessary from a school district's perspective. To further clarify this position, Colorado House Bill 08-1019 and Colorado Revised Statute 22-32-138 include a mandate that each local school district shall designate an employee of the school district to act as the CWEL. In lieu of designating an employee, a school district or the state charter school institute may contract with an individual to act as the CWEL. To find a CWEL by school district, please visit the CDE Foster Care Education webpage at www.cde.state.co.us. In addition, CDE employs a Foster Care Education State Coordinator to help navigate the laws, responsibilities, and training for CWELs. For other states, the CWEL position may be called something different. For the purposes of this guide, this school POC is referred to as CWEL throughout the text.

Furthermore, this section provides the effective procedures to utilize a CWEL position to the fullest potential without a significant increase in CWEL workload. CDE does not mandate specific procedures for this position, which leaves it open for a county to establish its own. However, not many school districts are defining this role, leaving it ambiguous and inconsistent. It is important for the action team to solidify CWEL procedures and responsibilities to standardize how the CWEL communicates and works with outside agencies. The creation and implementation of these procedures are a collaborative initiative between child welfare and juvenile justice. Ways in which outside agencies become involved can later be discussed if necessary.

Child Welfare Educational Planning Flow Chart

Below is the Educational Planning Flow Chart for Child Welfare (Figure 13.1). This procedural change assumes that the CWEL can send records. If information sharing and records transfer are a gap in service, it is encouraged that the CWEL work with school district records to streamline the process of sending records immediately upon notification. Furthermore, to fully implement these educational services, the school district administration and child welfare should reach an agreement on how to provide transportation to uphold the default decision to keep youth in the home school once removed from home until otherwise decided by the BID team.

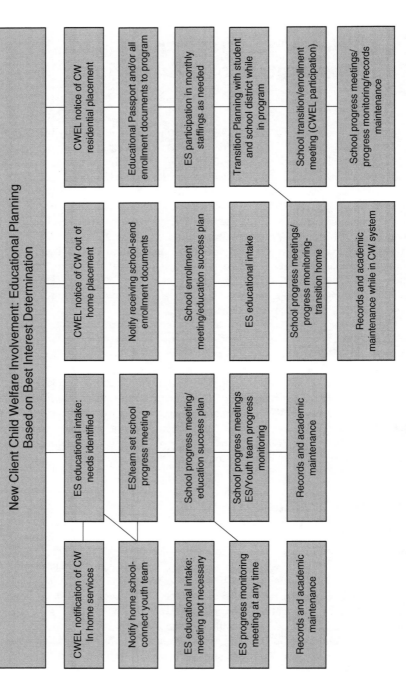

Figure 13.1 Child Welfare Educational Planning Flow Chart.

New Client Child Welfare Involvement: Educational Planning Based on Best Interest Determination

CWEL notification of CW In home services

Notify home school-connect youth team

ES educational intake: meeting not necessary

ES progress monitoring meeting at any time

Records and academic maintenance

ES educational intake: needs identified

ES/team set school progress meeting

School progress meeting/ education success plan

School progress meetings ES/Youth team progress monitoring

Records and academic maintenance

CWEL notice of CW out of home placement

Notify receiving school-send enrollment documents

School enrollment meeting/education success plan

ES educational intake

School progress meetings/ progress monitoring-transition home

Records and academic maintenance while in CW system

CWEL notice of CW residential placement

Educational Passport and/or all enrollment documents to program

ES participation in monthly staffings as needed

Transition Planning with student and school district while in program

School transition/enrollment meeting (CWEL participation)

School progress meetings/ progress monitoring/records maintenance

Intake only/progress monitoring

Best interest determination meeting stay in home school
Student not behind in classes or struggling with a particular subject area
Student has not experienced numerous school placements
Age and credits are on track with graduation guidelines

Enrolled and attending school
Student nor parent identify a need for educational planning
Good standing with school district (not expelled)
Parent engaged and advocate for youth

Home school progress meeting

Best interest determination stay in home school
Student indicated at risk factors for declining school behavior and/or attendance
Student identified one or more barriers in educational success
Assessment and/or parent identifying a need for a special education evaluation

Student may need a containment plan (if applicable)
Open truancy case and is receiving services through school
Student can benefit from school progress meeting for other reasons

New school enrollment meeting

Student removed from home and school
Not on track to receive credit for the year in current school
Student needs immediate enrollment in new school
Need to monitor progress while in foster care system and maintain school records

Open truancy case and/or not attending school of enrollment
Identified desire of school enrollment and re-engagement
Possible need for services such as tutoring, mentoring, or SPED

Residential care and transition planning

County places child in out of home placement
Records transfer and academic records maintained necessary
Repeated aggressive and/or unsafe behaviors on school grounds
No current enrollment in education program
Not on track to receive credit in current school
Need for services such as tutoring, mentoring, and/or mental health

Current expulsion
May or may not be special education
Open truancy case and/or not attending school of enrollment

Figure 13.1 Continued.

CWEL Child Welfare Sample Procedures

STEP ONE: School District Notification

STEP TWO: CWEL sends records to caseworker, supervising agency

STEP THREE: Assist in transportation to home school if youth removed from home

STEP FOUR: Participate in BID—Based on this decision take either step:

    A. Notify receiving school district CWEL by sending records and connect caseworker and ES; and

    B. Connect outside agency team with home school staff

STEP FIVE: Maintain database of child welfare notifications

STEP SIX: Assist in transition planning from residential placement or back into home school

Through the collaborative work in the action team, the CWEL can start with this sample and then modify these procedures to fit the need and resources. In this sample procedure, the CWEL receives a School District Notification of Involvement from child welfare. This notification triggers the CWEL to take action in the following ways depending on the notification information. The following are the various notification variations. These are the procedures on which the ES procedures in phase 3 are based.

It is important to note that anytime a youth is identified within special education, ensure CWEL and/or ES notifies special education departments both for home and receiving districts. Special education department staff ultimately makes the placement decisions based on Individualized Education Plan (IEP) service hours, least restrictive placement (LRE), services available, and in coordination with BID decisions.

Youth Remains in Home With In-Home Services

If the youth is not removed from home and is involved with in-home services through child welfare, the home school district CWEL notifies the current school and triggers any supports necessary to ensure the youth stays engaged and academically progresses. If the school indicates youth progress is declining at the start of the case, a school progress meeting is discussed immediately. Regardless of school meeting decision, due to the CWEL connecting all parties, the home school has contact information for the caseworker involved and the educational team is created including school staff, caseworker, GAL, and any other therapeutic contacts working with the family in the home. The CWEL notifies all parties during this time if the youth is special education or has a 504 plan and provides those documents to caseworker and ES. A school progress meeting can then be triggered by any team member at any time during the case with all members connected via email.

Due to the unknown outcome of the case, it is possible that the youth will be removed from the home and/or change schools in the future. For that reason, with parent/guardian permission, it is important to conduct an educational intake of the youth in the beginning of the case to establish a baseline of academic progress. This ensures timely intervention and/or transition into a new school if academics decline or other needs arise. At minimum, either the caseworker or ES should monitor progress in attendance and grades weekly or monthly if educational intake is not feasible for whatever reason. This regular academic monitoring ensures that it is quickly noticed if the youth declines academically. The caseworker can obtain school contact information from the CWEL to monitor progress.

Youth Removed from Home, Remain in Home School

At the time of notification, the youth is removed from the home, the CWEL collaborates with ES and/or the caseworker to quickly arrange a BID meeting of all team members to decide if the youth is to remain in home school with transportation or if the youth will be placed in a new school in line with the foster care home school district. Temporary transportation to home school is **crucial** in this situation and must be considered when writing procedures for how the CWEL and the ES will work together in arranging temporary transportation. Best practice is to address transportation either before or at the time of new foster placement, which may include both temporary and sustainable solutions to ensure the youth is provided with reliable transport to the home school. The CWEL notifies all parties during this time if the youth is special education or has a 504 plan and provides both general and special education documents to ES and/or the child welfare caseworker. The CWEL notifies home school that the youth might be late to arrive due to transportation from a new home the next day. It is best practice to have this meeting as quickly as possible so as not to delay home school continuation or new school enrollment. The goal is to eliminate any possible time a youth spends outside of school unenrolled. If the youth is placed in a facility, the default decision should be to provide transportation from the facility to the home school unless otherwise notified. In Colorado, facilities can utilize funding to assist with this effort if appropriate for youth to attend home school and not the on-grounds facility school. For some, this might not always be appropriate.

If the BID team decides that the student stays in home school, the CWEL follows up with home school to provide ongoing support in current environment while taking into context the trauma that child has experienced due to removal from the home. Initially, the email connection was set by the CWEL. As a result, anyone on the youth's team can quickly initiate a school progress meeting for the youth at home school to ensure all education needs are met while the youth is in care. The CWEL sends all educational enrollment documents to the caseworker who keeps these documents in electronic format. These documents complete a youth's educational passport and include:

- Transcript
- Birth certificate
- Immunizations
- Attendance

- Behavior
- SPED records
- Any expulsion letter
- 504 plan

An educational passport is designed to be the cover sheet listing all school placements and enrollment documents included in the file. All of these records should be given to the parent and/or foster parent upon receipt along with the caseworker. With the education passport, the foster parent/guardian simply needs to provide proof of residency and custody order at time of enrollment. Due to CWEL contact, the receiving CWEL can notify the new receiving school of incoming youth enrollment. Even if the foster parent does not have records, the youth immediately enrolls and the CWEL triggers the records to be sent within the ten day timeframe. The actual education passport document may or may not be useful for all counties.

Special Consideration

Day Treatment: If home school is a special education placement in a day treatment setting determined by home district of youth, then home district should already be providing transportation to the day treatment facility. In this scenario, transportation to day treatment until otherwise determined is **crucial** in maintaining a special education youth in the day treatment setting. When the home district CWEL is notified, he/she should immediately call the receiving district CWEL to work out transportation arrangements. It could be that new district is willing to assist in transportation as it would be more financially possible for receiving district. However, this is not a guarantee. If the BID meeting decides the youth is to stay in home day treatment, transportation will, if anything, be the responsibility of special education departments within the home school district and child welfare. Education costs are to the home district in which parent resides. If parents cannot be found, the last known address is used. Any disputes or discussions about educational billing typically start at the home and receiving school districts' Special Education Out of District Coordinator positions. Transportation in the interim of this decision is critical. Make best efforts to find a foster parent and/or ask caseworkers to transport before placing youth in ANY home.

Special Consideration

Kinship Care: If a youth is removed from one parent and sent to live with the other or a relative and staying in home school, it is suggested to make contact with receiving family before providing any additional services. BID meetings are still necessary in kinship care. If a parent or relative is adjusted to be a co-parent or guardian and the youth is already comfortable living with this person, immediate service may not be necessary but rather academic monitoring. However, even in this situation, if the receiving parent or relative describes educational difficulties, then the ES proceeds immediately with a new case for educational services.

If the youth does not know receiving parent or relative, it is suggested that ES still contact this parent first before providing any additional services. Youth and family may have a difficult time adjusting and potentially need direct educational services as well. If either of these placements do not fit for youth, it is important that ES still has an educational file on the youth in the case of a move.

Youth Removed from Home and Removed from Home School

Should the BID decision be for the youth to be removed from home school and enrolled in a new school, then the goal is to eliminate any possible time a youth spends outside of school unenrolled. Temporary transportation to home school is important in this situation until the youth moves to a new school. Best practice is to ensure that new foster placement or another party can provide transport to home school until sustainable transportation is in place for the youth to start in a new school the immediate next school day. Serious consideration should be made in considering the timing of a school move based on the school calendar, particularly for high school age youth.

If the action team is establishing the ES position described in phase 3, upon receipt of notification, the ES can create an educational passport with all the documents, give the documents to foster parents, conduct an education intake, determine the level of need for services, update the educational passport file, conduct educational meetings, monitor attendance and academics, and keep the youth's education intact, despite any further moves. The ES conducts any future BID meetings, school progress meetings, and/or educational service planning necessary while the youth is in out of home care and further expands individual education planning. This process is discussed in more depth in phase 3.

Special Consideration

Day Treatment New Placement: In the instance when the youth is removed from the home and school and the new district makes a determination for placement in day treatment, it is critical to maintain transportation to home school until a new day treatment is found for the youth. Moving a youth to day treatment can take time, and the expectation is that the youth remains enrolled in school until the day treatment placement is secured. The special education team from both home and the receiving district must be involved in this process.

Kinship Care: If a youth moves in with another parent or a relative's home *and moves schools*, it is suggested that ES contact the parent first to obtain approval from the receiving parent or relative to provide educational services that follows directions as mentioned above for kinship care placement. This will also give a good amount of background information on the youth to determine the next steps and the support needed in the new school setting.

CWEL Juvenile Justice Sample Procedures

As a result of the action team, all juvenile justice staff have a CWEL as the direct school district point of contact so as to trigger the inclusion of home school staff in the juvenile justice youth team. The outlined procedures for the CWEL will look different based on the placement of the youth at the time of notification. The CWEL has the ability to look up school progress, send academic records to the emerging youth team, and connect via email the home school staff with the supervising agent to coordinate efforts to support and/or re-engage the youth in the school environment. If the youth is seeking re-enrollment into a school district, the supervising agency can utilize the CWEL to determine school options based on academic history and current status. Given that there are other options available outside of the school district, it is best to coordinate with an ES for educational services as well. If no ES is present in the county, the CWEL can maintain a comprehensive list of educational settings available in and outside the district. Action team members can assist in keeping this list accurate as well. For example, if a new charter school moves into the area and works well with at-risk youth, perhaps the director of the program could be invited to an action team meeting to further collaborate.

CWEL involvement may be short-term but provides crucial contact information and connection to records when necessary. The CWEL can maintain a simple Excel database for the first year at a minimum, which documents all the names of youth where notification is received. This provides a simple way to document youth involved in outside systems and in receipt of CWEL specific services to track how many juvenile justice youth exist in the school district and what supports are needed most often. This database should include the youth's name, date of birth, notifying agency, SPED status, services offered, and follow-up data on academic standing. The CWEL may designate a school case manager, administrator, liaison, mental health, and/or social worker with the task of monitoring academic progress at the building level. This is helpful because the school staff will then be able to check-in on these students and if progress declines, the school can easily notify the youth team and suggest the next steps. The process and database then allow for the tracking of positive outcomes such as improvements in attendance, grades, and grade-level progression. This database tracks court-involved youth and can provide reasons for the allocation of funding for further supportive positions given the number of court-involved youth and the services necessary to keep youth engaged.

Research indicates identifiers when youth are at risk for dropping out and a CWEL or designated school staff can more quickly identify present school at-risk factors. Once a youth is involved in the juvenile justice system, it is important to monitor these key factors for school so as to intervene if youth academic status is reflective of a youth at risk. To that end, a CWEL can review academic records and put in place supports to eliminate the risk of dropout based on the common signs. Indicating factors include attendance below 80% in eighth or ninth grade, a GPA less than 2.0, failing a core academic area in ninth grade, and/or multiple discipline infractions. These academic factors are shown to result in a youth dropping out of high school or not graduating on time with same age peers (Burke, 2015). With regard to specific risk factors, it was shown in a study out of Oregon that "students' attendance, achievement, and behavior have stronger relationships with graduating than do their race/ethnicity and their achievement on state testing in reading and math" (Burke, 2015, p. 2). School districts may also have their own local data around dropout early warning risk factors that they may want to apply to screen youth who become systems involved. When designing CWEL juvenile justice procedures, the action team may want to list these identifying factors when determining how and what action a CWEL takes given current academic status.

Juvenile Justice Educational Planning Flow Chart

Figure 13.2 on the next page provides an outline of juvenile justice educational planning procedures.

CWEL Sample Procedures

STEP ONE: School District Notification of Juvenile Justice Involvement Receipt
STEP TWO (A): Juvenile sent home with/without supervision
STEP TWO (B): Juvenile sent to detention
STEP THREE: CWEL review records, notify school designee, CWEL database entry
  A. No services necessary, monitor progress, notify of any academic decline
  B. Services necessary, CWEL notifies ES and/or supervising agency
  C. Parent contact, school meeting, academic monitoring
STEP FOUR: Juvenile sent to out of home/residential placement
  A. CWEL/registrar send records to ES for education passport
  B. CWEL receive notification of 30–60 days prior to expected transition date
  C. CWEL/school designee attend transition staffing
  D. School enrollment meeting/actions for enrollment as deemed necessary
  E. School and ES monitor progress, notify of any academic decline
STEP FIVE: Supervising agency connects with school staff on any future concerns

These procedures reflect the process by which a home district CWEL receives a School District Notification of Juvenile Justice Involvement form via email from the juvenile assessment center within 24 hours of assessment decision. This notification triggers the CWEL to look up student records, review academic standing, and enter information into the CWEL database. Depending on youth placement as a result of assessment, and the school review of records, determines the next action steps. Those actions steps are described in detail below. If there is an ES, the involvement of such persons is described within this flow of information as well.

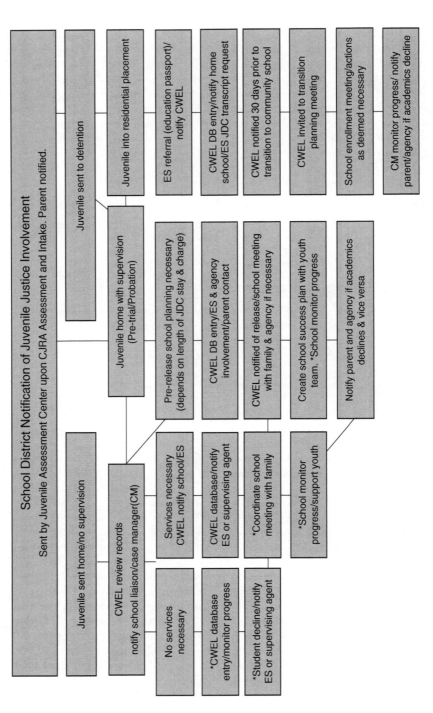

Figure 13.2 Juvenile Justice Educational Planning Flow Chart.

Home school with supervision no educational services

Supervising agency notified and have no concerns
Student not behind in classes or struggling with a particular subject area
Student has not experienced numerous school placements
Age and credits are on track with graduation guidelines
School meeting can be triggered by any youth team member as case continues

Enrolled and attending school
Student nor parent identify a need for educational planning
Good standing with school district (not expelled)
Parent engaged and advocate for youth
Neither student nor parent want services

Home school with supervision and educational services

Supervising agency has academic concerns
Student records show declining school behavior and/or attendance
Parent/school identified one or more barriers in educational success
Agency and/or parent identifying a need for a Special Education evaluation
Can benefit from socio/emotional supports in school

Student may need a ISMP plan (if applicable)
Open truancy case and is receiving services through school
Student can benefit from School Progress Meeting for other reasons
Referral to ES

Detention planning with school district/home school

Supervising, school or parent has academic concerns
Not on track to receive credit for the year in current school
Student records show declining behavior and/or attendance
Student needs immediate enrollment upon release
Need to maintain school records by supervising agency due to high mobility
Referral to ES

Open truancy case and/or not attending school of enrollment
May have current or pending expulsion
Identified desire of school enrollment and re-engagement
Possible need for services such as tutoring, mentoring, or SPED
Need for collaboration with outside agency

Residential placement/transition planning

County places child in out of home placement
Records transfer and academic records maintained by supervising agency
Repeated aggressive and/or unsafe behaviors on school grounds
No current enrollment in education program
Not on track to graduate on time based on credits
Need for services such as tutoring, mentoring, and/or mental health

May have current expulsion
May or may not be special education either ED or LD
Open truancy case and/or not attending school of enrollment
Agency/parent has academic concerns returning to school
Referral for ES

Key terms:

ES: Education Direct Service staff
CWEL: Child Welfare Education Liaison
DB: Database
CM: Case Manager or Liaison providing direct service

Figure 13.2 Continued.

Youth Returns to Home with Supervision and Home School with No Direct Educational Services

If the CWEL reviews the academic record and has no academic concerns at the time of notification, he/she may decide that no academic services are necessary at the time of notification. Reasoning to sustain from educational intervention includes:

- Youth is on track by age/grade level;
- Youth is enrolled and attending school;
- Youth is in good standing with school district;
- Parent is engaged;
- Youth has not experienced numerous school placements;
- Youth/parent decline educational services.

At this time, the CWEL enters information into the database and designates a member of the school staff to monitor progress. Should academic performance decline, the CWEL or designated school staff contact the parent, ES, and/or supervising agency to trigger a collaborative effort to support youth. At this time, any preventative services at the school level should be considered based on resources such as mentoring, school-based therapy, peer mentoring, and clubs/activities/sports in individual schools that can support keeping the youth engaged. Professionals cannot afford not to offer preventative services given what has already been mentioned regarding recidivism. Typically, this is not considered and it is truly a paradigm shift from the traditional reactive approach to the more beneficial preventative approach.

Youth Returns to Home with Supervision and Home School with Direct Educational Services

If the CWEL reviews academic record and has academic concern, the CWEL notifies the supervising agency and/or ES. Reasons to initiate educational services include but are not limited to:

- Youth needing an ISMP due to a sex offense;
- Youth has truancy involvement;
- Youth is not on track to graduate based on age/credit;
- Youth has behavioral or attendance issues;
- Youth or parent indicates that additional resources are needed.

At this time, the CWEL enters information into the database, designates a school staff member to collaborate with outside agencies to participate in a school meeting, offer supports, and jointly review progress. The ES is a partner in this as that person can connect all the professionals to the school staff to create the youth team. If the youth continues to struggle, the newly formed youth team collaborates on the next steps with full family involvement. If youth academics improve, progress is monitored in the hope of no further juvenile justice involvement. These youth may go through periods of doing really well to times of struggle and it will often be necessary to monitor progress consistently at the school level, continue supportive services, and maintain continued enrollment despite setbacks.

Youth Goes into Detention with Pre-Release Educational Planning

First and foremost for youth that are on track in school when placed in detention, encourage parents to pick up work at school to stay on track. The CWEL can request from home school that a packet of work be prepared for the youth to complete while in detention. While the youth is in detention, the CWEL reviews academic records. If there are academic concerns voiced by any party, including the CWEL, supervising agency, ES, or parent, educational planning is initiated. The same academic concerns listed above are reason for pre-release academic planning while the youth is in detention. Joint planning is particularly important if an offense occurred on school grounds as there may be placement changes or disciplinary measures. The length of time a youth is in detention is considered when determining the level of educational planning necessary. If a youth is enrolled but not academically progressing, joint educational planning can commence to prepare for a release back into current school. However, if the youth is on track academically in the current school, the CWEL notifies the school designee to contact the parent and supervising agency for a possible school meeting upon return to home school. If lack of time before release prevents a school meeting from occurring, at minimum, school staff can check in with a youth upon return to get the youth back on track with classes. If the youth is not otherwise enrolled in public school, the ES will work with family, supervising agency, and possibly the CWEL to further educationally plan for the youth considering all educational options in/out of the school district.

Youth Goes into Out of Home Care/Residential Treatment with Education/Transition Planning

While the youth is in detention and placement is determined, the supervising agency makes the request to ES for academic records and the education passport. The CWEL and/or records designee sends records to ES, enters information into the CWEL database, notifies home school, and awaits notification from ES/supervising agency of a 30–60-day transition meeting. The ES discusses with family and team either during the monthly staff meeting or beforehand. The CWEL role will depend on if the youth is going back to home school or needs help selecting a new school within the district. If youth is deemed special education, the school district special education coordinator will need to be involved to discuss specific options available under special education. Oftentimes, the CWEL is the initial contact and connects team with appropriate school staff to participate in the youth team. There will certainly be academic concerns to be addressed by the entire youth team and planning will ensure a smooth transition back into community schools with as limited time as possible in between the placement discharge and the start of new school. CWELs may or may not be a part of this process depending on the community school selection of charter, public or private. In the following chapters, education transition planning is described more in depth.

Chapter 14

Improvements in System Procedures

This section reviews two processes in which multiple systems must coordinate. Often times, particular processes see gaps in educational service for many counties in Colorado so they are formalized here.

Best Interest Determinations

As mentioned previously, per the Every Student Succeeds Act (ESSA), BID mandates necessitate both child welfare and the school district to collaborate on transportation to home school to maintain educational stability. The review of county processes for BID meetings is the first step in improving this system procedure. As a team, facilitate a discussion about the child welfare intake process and how BID meetings are currently occurring in each case. Furthermore, do not forget to include BID processes when a youth is removed and placed in kinship care or from foster home to foster home. Oftentimes, this process is overlooked, however, foster youth may be very engaged in home school of a foster home and a best interest determination is crucial at this point in the process. It is often assumed a foster youth will move schools if moving foster homes and this should not be the default decision. Additionally, it is required that the same BID shall take place for kinship care placements. Every single school move is important and should be handled with care by giving it the attention it deserves.

Once the action team reviews county wide procedures, draft a BID flow chart documenting where school district notification should occur and, if an ES is in place, how that notification will occur to this position as mentioned in the first part of this phase. BID processes are mentioned here because the notifications in place for all child welfare and juvenile justice cases will automatically trigger a BID meeting if notification indicates an out of home removal occurred. Establishing a clear protocol for BID will automatically place education needs as a top priority in the beginning of the case. Design and/or improve the BID flow chart to reflect both emergency and non-emergency removals to show how each differs for education purposes. This flow chart should also include the steps done by child welfare to ensure the county is in line with the ESSA mandate that the default decision for both emergency and non-emergency out of home removals is for youth to stay in home school and transportation be provided until otherwise notified. The specific way in which child welfare ensures that this transportation is arranged for every case needs to be finalized.

Clarification and consistency ensure that the BID meeting occurs within timeframe requirements with all parties after the youth is removed. This also assists the count attorney's role in how they will send official notification of removal to schools for legal purposes. Be sure to include all agencies in the flow chart that have involvement in this process including all other legal agencies (see list below). For emergency removals, an additional change in process can be inserted when the judge or magistrate receives the initial notification phone call and asks education specific questions when deciding to order the emergency home removal. This information is also helpful for the BID meeting. In later court hearings, judges and magistrates can also incorporate educational questioning to assist in keeping education as a priority in the case. This process can be implemented immediately before any new procedure training and will initiate case workers to be more conscious of educational information because they know the court will inquire. As a result, the change in process can occur at a minimum of three points:

- Initial decision of placement: Supervisor email notification to CWEL and ES; including youth and placement information.
- Judge/Magistrate order: Educational questioning when approving a home removal and during review hearings. Court documents submitted for review hearings can be revised to include an education specific section if it is not included already.
- County Attorney filing: Official notification of removal to school, CWEL, and ES if necessary.

Roles and Responsibilities for Best Interest Determinations

To better understand the roles and responsibilities of individual agencies identified in the flow chart, below is a review of all agencies involved and individual roles as it relates to education.

Child welfare caseworker: Notifies judge/magistrate, ES, and the CWEL of removal from home. The caseworker is responsible for coordinating immediate temporary transportation to home school the next day after removal from home, often with assistance from the ES and CWEL. The caseworker also makes the best decision for the youth to attend school the next day based on emotional state and varying factors.

ER removal: Supervisor provides immediate notification to school district CWEL and ES and written notification within 24–48 hours to trigger a BID meeting. Via phone, caseworker answers specific education questions from the Judge or Magistrate. Temporary transportation is provided.

Non-emergency removal: Written notification is provided to the school district CWEL prior to removal to trigger a BID meeting. (Example: It is possible to conduct a family progress meeting with all parties to make a decision of placement and the school district CWEL can be included in this process.)

Judge/magistrate: Complete a removal order form via phone for ER placements and ask specific education placement questions when issuing an order.

CWEL: The CWEL can send records to ES and/or caseworker as well as notifying the home school of child welfare involvement or send records to new receiving school CWEL based on the BID decision. If staying in home school, the CWEL coordinates transportation to home school.

Home school staff: With notification, provide feedback to the CWEL of academic standing and current academic functioning such as attendance, grade level, and discipline.

ES: Once notification is received, creates educational file, schedules BID meeting, and conducts educational intake either before or after the BID meeting to determine level of need for education services.

Probation/pre-trial/diversion (crossover youth): Participate in BID meeting and provide any feedback and terms of supervision.

GAL, therapist, county attorney, district attorney, CASA (any other individuals involved in youth case): Participate in BID meetings to offer unique perspective based on role in case.

Examples in Practice

For Douglas County, the team chose to revise a current notification form to reflect specific contact information for agency staff to complete the school district notification of child welfare involvement. For now, this notification email is sent to the school district on youth for whom out of home placement notification is occurring. Ideally, it is recommended that notification is sent for any youth involved with child welfare and action teams are encouraged to work toward this goal to ensure education planning at every single point of systems entry. In Douglas County, for out of home removal, this notification triggers a BID meeting and possible school supports at home school. Douglas County created the ES position titled Educational Navigator and this notice, once received, triggers the Educational Navigator to further create an educational file on the youth, commence all educational services, and ensure the BID occurs.

Education Transition Procedures

A fundamental piece of this framework lies in systems, families, and schools partnering for successful transition planning. This collaboration is crucial to the academic success of court-involved youth. Many facilities will have transition coordinators. In order to best partner with facilities, action teams must align and identify, in writing, the roles and responsibilities of outside agencies with the partnership of the facility transition coordinator. If there is no transition coordinator in the facility, it can be the responsibility of the ES (identified in phase 3) or the child welfare case worker to lead the youth teams in transition and coordinate the exchange of information to ensure seamless transitions. Either way, the action team should identify this lead and put it in writing for procedural manuals and future training.

Schools often feel as though they operate in a vacuum and do not have the support of outside agencies when dealing with troubled youth, particularly when not given enough information about incoming new students. All too often, informational barriers exist that make it difficult to share information on a youth in the child welfare and/or justice system, which is crucial in times of education transition. Following the implementation found in phase 1, the action team should have addressed that barrier and can move forward on building the individual relationships between systems and schools during education transition. The relationship between child welfare to school and juvenile justice to school will look different. With the commitment of collaboration, the process of giving/receiving information established and the action team in place, it is time to look at how each agency/school can help each other ultimately better serve youth amidst multiple transitions.

Together, schools and agencies can coordinate school and individual interventions, promoting positive reinforcement that targets the root cause of behaviors identified in individual cases. Many transitioning youth will need this type of approach to re-engage successfully. At the local level, action teams now have a cross-agency collaboration to engage all systems to improve transitions. Families also play a large role in this process and should be included in any planning to keep a youth enrolled and attending once transitioned into a community school. Other agencies such as CASA, youth advocate programs, mentoring, and tutoring programs within the community should be tapped as a resource partner at this time. Coordinate with these programs to offer individual support in every plan created by a youth team. The more school staff feels they have support from these outside agencies to address specific behavioral and academic needs, the more willing an entire school will be in supporting the youth coming in to their school. With the introduction of informal cross-agency training, school staff will know who to contact and when, the roles of the outside supervising agencies, the resources those agencies offer, and vice versa. When teachers are informed and included in this transition process, they can support youth more individually by monitoring academic progress, providing weekly updates, giving immediate feedback to youth in the classroom, and overall build a nurturing positive adult relationship in a school setting (Ronsekranz et al., 2014).

Transitions occur for youth in both systems quite often. Unfortunately, while the literature is clear on transition recommendations for juvenile justice youth from long-term residential facilities to community schools, there is not much information on the more common education transitions of child welfare and juvenile justice youth. More specifically, two areas in need of improvement are child welfare multiple community school transitions and short-term detention stays for juvenile justice youth. For juvenile justice youth, this lack of literature may be a result of the assumption that most states have school districts that maintain current youth enrollment in home school while in detention so as to keep youth on track. This is not always the case in Colorado. Youth are often enrolled into the school district in which the detention center is located. Child welfare youth can experience significant transitions into new schools based on kinship /foster home placement or residential schools when a foster home cannot be located. Given the federally mandated BID procedures, the change in schools for child welfare youth should decrease in the next few years. However, circumstances will arise that will dictate a youth changing schools regardless. More importantly, the education transitions experienced by juvenile justice and crossover youth need standardization across the state of Colorado and perhaps many others.

Review of Current Procedures

To this end, the action team or an appointed sub-committee should take the time to review all transition planning procedures that currently exist for all types of transition that can occur in a youth's life span. This includes transition school programs for elementary to middle school youth, eighth to ninth grade, transition planning from a corrections commitment, high school to college transition, and so on. Begin to document, from these existent procedures, the aspects that are most helpful to include for educational transitions experienced by court-involved youth. Take time to meet with both ongoing caseworkers and youth in transition caseworkers to discover what tools, documentation, and planning model staff are utilizing to transition a youth from school to school or residential facility back into community school. If no formal model exists in the agencies, gather whatever resources are currently being used, utilize staff feedback, and integrate into the new transitions procedure to keep caseworkers engaged and involved in the process of standardizing procedures. The initial transition procedures for 17th Judicial District youth were designed utilizing special education transition procedures and documents that included important details and steps that were also necessary for court-involved youth. The 17th Judicial District Education Advocate also took time to interview school staff, transition coordinators, education directors, and others who significantly contributed to all types of education transitions. There is no need to re-create the wheel but rather build on what is successfully utilized in the field currently. Blend the procedures, information, documents, and feedback with the following sample procedures to draft new and improved education transition planning procedures specific to the county.

Facilities are operating with their own individual transition procedures that include an education component when necessary. However, many locally run detention facilities do not have a transition program specifically addressing education and most youth transitioning from detention are of school age and must seek school enrollment upon discharge per court order. Any time a youth is removed from school for a significant amount of time, even if only a week while in detention, academic consequences can ensue. With the foundation of action team collaboration in place, standardizing all types of transitions processes will not seem as daunting as it once was. There are three suggested ways of initiating this process depending on level of collaboration by facilities and the size of the county. If this guide is being implemented in an urban county where a variety of residential facilities and detentions are utilized, maybe consider the first option below. Perhaps counties can bring in the most readily used facilities to collaborate into a brainstorm session within the action team. In smaller counties, option two might suit the action team best. Facilities work with many different counties and agencies, some might find it easier to formalize a county specific procedure and then notify the facilities of the changes. An additional option would be to partner with the facility most utilized in the county and formalize procedures with that facility first and disperse changes to other facilities once finalized. The options are outlined below:

OPTION ONE: Formalize transition procedures within the county and notify detention and facilities of the expectations of the county.

OPTION TWO: Partner with all facility education directors by inviting them to an action team meeting and brainstorm collaboratively to define transitions procedures.

OPTION THREE: Partner with the most readily used facility in the county to formalize transition procedures, keeping in mind specific differences that may exist between facilities. Once finalized, begin to train other facilities on the county transition procedures to standardize every education transition scenario between schools, facilities, and detention facilities.

KEY EDUCATION TRANSITION PROCEDURAL QUESTIONS

Identify, step by step, where educational planning exists within all processes of transition.

Identify current documentation utilized in the field for transitions.

Identify any formal procedures for school to school transitions.

Identify all education transitions in need of formalized planning.

Review the Transition Summary document.

Review sample transition procedures.

Meet with transition coordinators of residential and day treatment facilities.

Meet with detention facility education director.

Meet with agency staff to identify gaps in service in education transition.

Identify school resources available for transitioning youth.

School Resources in Education Transition

Schools may have resources such as school-based therapists, peer mentors, and social workers along with the flexibility in scheduling and other supportive programming to assist in easing any type of education transition. Within the action team, identify who is working particularly well in the individual schools and what positive and successful strategies they use to re-engage youth. Invite those schools to an action team meeting to inform outside agencies and the CWEL of what is currently in place to integrate youth into community schools upon transition. This is a way to align schools with agencies in implementing education transition procedures that will foster timely communication, collaboration, and enrollment. Additionally, it is important to incorporate credit recovery options as the youth may be at an academic credit deficit upon step down.

Roles and Responsibilities in Transition Procedures

These responsibilities are specific to educational transition. It is often found that systems and school staff do not know what their role is in this process and/or how they can help. At times, there is confusion about who is notifying the school district of transition plans and the notification is not received in time to plan effectively. The purpose of outlining transition planning in the county is to ensure that never again is there a failure to notify the home school district of the transition of a youth. This is a comprehensive list and should be adapted to fit the specific county. If there is not an ES working in the county, take those appointed responsibilities out of the county roles when drafting county specific procedures. This is a process that, once again, will need to be introduced to direct service staff of all agencies with flow charts and written documentation detailing the roles and responsibilities of each agency/school with continued encouragement to adhere to the new procedures to avoid duplication of services.

CWEL/School Responsibility:

- Provide discipline information including behavior history, expulsion status, attendance, and behavior contracts for placement to ES and/or caseworker.
- Assist in smooth school transitions by actively participating in staffing to set the tone of expectations or options for a return to community school.
- At initial placement decision, advocate for the youth to attend home school while in residential placement if in best interest.
- Ensure IEP and SPED documentation is up to date and participate in SPED meetings conducted in placement.
- Respond timely to SPED evaluation requests from facility schools.
- Appoint a school staff member to report any attendance or behavior concerns to the youth team once back in community school.
- School safety for client and ALL youth in school including creating any type of safety plans if necessary.
- Connecting youth to school staff that can foster relationships with positive peers and adults.

- Participate or appoint staff to participate in a residential transition planning meeting to review options for the youth in returning to community schools.
- If not available to participate in staffings, communicate with ES on updates and educational options.
- Provide transition documents from facility to new school staff and review together so staff have a better understanding of youth's current functioning.

Other Important School Staff:

Special Education Out of District Coordinators: This position is responsible for SPED youth transition in and out of district schools from residential facilities and has much experience with transition planning already. Coordinators also are responsible for requesting educational funding for youth in residential facilities. It is necessary to include this position for all special education youth in transition to determine step down placement. This is also the staff that a CWEL will connect to the youth team when a SPED evaluation is requested while in long-term placement. These coordinators should also be notified if the youth is in short-term detention stay.

Student Services Director/Intervention Services: When there are youth disciplinary measures in place preventing enrollment into a public school setting such as an expulsion, these staff should be contacted to review what options are available during expulsion once a youth is ready to transition out of either short-term detention stays or longer-term residential placements. These staff can also oversee the creation of any plan created for juveniles with sexual offenses.

Agency Responsibility:

For foster youth: Child welfare case worker

For juvenile justice youth: Probation or parole officer (if no child welfare involved in placement)

For crossover youth: Child welfare case worker (These responsibilities can be assigned to ES)

- Keep all enrollment documents in a central location amidst transitions.
- Keep ES apprised in facility staffing.
- Lead facilitation of ISMP meeting for youth with sexual offenses when transitioning from facility.
- Give school contact/CWEL advanced notice of 30–60 days of transition as often as possible.
- Give youth teams notice if youth goes into detention and expectancy of stay and/or next steps.
- Give school overview of how agencies will remain involved once youth discharges from facility.
- Establish a group email for youth team upon re-entry into community school and include parents as well.
- Engage parents in transition planning within the first week of a youth being placed in facility.

Guardian Ad Litem (GAL) Responsibility:

- Communicate educational needs of the individual youth to facility school.
- Advocate for appropriate education services and assessment in facilities.
- Participation and feedback on appropriateness of transition planning from facility schools.
- Act as an Educational Surrogate Parent if the youth needs an adult to maintain educational signing rights.
- Advocate for youth to stay in home school and transportation be provided if facility school is not appropriate.

Parent/Guardian Responsibility:

- Sign release of information at point of intake for all general and special education records.
- Attend all facility staffing and school enrollment meetings.
- Educate themselves on special education and take advantage of training resources.
- Engage in active collaboration and communication as soon as youth leaves home.
- If necessary, take the lead on making the written request for a formal special education evaluation to facility.
- Ensure that the youth is connected with community resources and mental health upon step down including continued access to health care and medications.
- Participate as a valuable decision maker in the transition planning.
- Take youth potential school visits when youth is home on pass and before discharge.
- Take the lead on submitting all enrollment paperwork for the new school.
- Maintain own educational file on youth with all enrollment paperwork and educational history.
- Utilize direct contact with new community school staff and actively participate on the youth team.

Youth Responsibility:

- Create their education history and be empowered to maintain all of their own educational documents if the parent is not engaged.
- Communicate academic needs to the new facility school.
- Advocate for self to participate in pro-social groups and/or sports at school upon step down.
- Identify own transition goals and actively participate in creating a transition plan.

Facility Responsibility:

- The education director maintains and distributes relevant educational needs and academic history to facility education staff.

- Conduct special education evaluations if requested.
- Educational progress reports each month for staffing.
- Coordinate a pre-transition meeting before youth exits facility.
- Completion of a transition summary or the like at the time of transition for receiving school.
- Transition coordinator works directly with county ES and the youth team to establish educational transition plan.
- Creation of transition plan document in coordination with the youth team and ES.
- Send facility records and final transcript to ES, parent, and new school.

ES Responsibility:

The ES role is defined in detail in phase 3. These responsibilities are specific to education transition and take some of the responsibilities off the direct agency staff:

- Address academic need and goals at first facility staffing.
- Coordinating with education director and/or transition coordinator for transition planning staffing and invite school staff of home school district to participate.
- Ensuring the transition summary document and final transcript is completed and given to community school staff preferably prior to discharge.
- Sending record and final transcript to new school upon transition.
- Coordinating school meetings and enrollments in line with school calendar.
- Assisting the parent in transition planning and visit potential schools.

Brief Summary of Step-by-Step Procedures

CWELs are helpful during transition in/out of detentions, facilities, and/or foster home school placements. For longer residential stays, it is the responsibility of the outside agencies (child welfare or juvenile justice) to verify receiving parent/guardian home address and school district first, this is to determine which school district shall be notified of impending transition. Staff can utilize online tools on school district websites to verify home district based on current address. Next, for longer residential stays, agencies should give a 30–60 day notice to the home school district CWEL of the youth ready to transition back into community school. Schools also recognize that this timeline will not always be possible but is certainly best practice to ensure immediate enrollment upon step down from placement. The CWEL requests the residential facility or current school from which foster youth will transition to complete a Transition Summary in preparation for transition and request transition staffing. The CWEL may work with current school staff, transition coordinator of facility, ES, or other mental health staff to present all receiving school district options, timelines, and eligibility for enrollment. This process should look very similar to what the residential facilities are doing already when a youth is special education. A transition plan is typically done in facilities, but not always by community schools, so this may be a new procedural implementation that will need a lot of support in the introduction to ensure it becomes a standard of practice. The sample Transition Summary goes into academic detail by including strengths/weaknesses, academic levels, staff recommendations, and so on. For facilities, if no type of transition document is filled out prior to the transition staffing, perhaps it can be completed during a transition specific staffing. For community schools, this document should be filled out before the youth moves schools, which may or may not include transition staffing. The transition summary can then be utilized during a school enrollment meeting and/or by the ES to inform receiving school district of academic needs. How the action team plans to implement new transition procedures will depend on how this document is adapted and utilized. The action team may use the sample Transition Summary document in the Appendix and adapt it to fit the county needs. Please note that this form can be completed in electronic format for ease of use. Typically, the transition coordinator, therapist, education director, social worker, or the school teacher can complete a transition document easily if not the transition coordinator.

Note while reviewing these child welfare education procedures that child welfare youth experience multiple community school transitions and these procedures should be relevant for all types of school moves. In addition, it takes into consideration that the BID process is in place, but not every county in every state is practicing this new mandate consistently. That is why it is important to review the aforementioned BID example procedures first before discussing how to improve transition procedures. If practice is in place to notify the CWEL with each move as described, the CWEL will also be able to initiate these meetings, thus helping to establish consistency across systems. Be mindful that even if a youth is attending school in a foster home, if the youth is doing well in this school, efforts should be considered to keep this youth in that school until an appropriate time to move occurs or the BID decision is made, thus making education transitions unnecessary. It is inappropriate to not consider school placement stability just because it is the home school of a foster placement. There is always a chance for a youth to connect to that school and all efforts should be made to keep those connections intact as long as possible and potentially eliminate a school move. The same CWEL notification procedures and below transition procedures outlined in this phase should take place for every school move so as to initiate the same school supports in each school. Every effort should be made at the new school to connect with a school administrator, support the youth in entering into new classrooms, and ensure the youth is integrated in a way that avoids the youth feeling isolated or behind in that new classroom. All of these points are listed in Chapter 15.

Step-by-Step Transition Procedure: Child Welfare

STEP ONE: Transfer educational records to new community or facility school.
STEP TWO: Establish transition and education goals along with treatment goals in first staffing.

STEP THREE: Keep education planning on the forefront of the agenda with every staffing.

STEP FOUR: Notify receiving CWEL at a minimum of 30–60 days of transition date.

STEP FIVE: Hold a transition planning meeting with CWEL participation (and/or ES participation).

STEP SIX: Assist family in coordinating school meetings and enrollments. Some schools may require information sessions or orientation attendance, interviews, and so on, and should be coordinated with the team while the youth is on home passes or spending time with on return to the guardian/parent.

STEP SEVEN (without ES): Verify with the CWEL of new school enrollment and start date.

STEP EIGHT (without ES): Connect the youth team via email with school staff with assistance of the CWEL to monitor progress.

STEP NINE (without ES): Schedule school meeting with youth team at school if situation declines.

OR

STEP SEVEN (with ES): Create an Education Success Plan with the youth and school at a school enrollment meeting once the youth steps down out of facility school.

STEP EIGHT (with ES): Set a school progress meeting with the team and connect all parties via team email.

STEP NINE (with ES): Check attendance weekly and monitor progress.

STEP TEN (with ES): Continue school progress meetings as decided by youth team.

Step-by-Step Transition Procedure: Juvenile Justice

STEP ONE: Transfer educational records to facility school.

STEP TWO: Establish transition and education goals along with treatment goals in first staffing.

STEP THREE: Keep transition planning on the forefront of the team with every staffing.

STEP FOUR: Notify CWEL between 30–60 days of transition date.

STEP FIVE: Hold a transition planning meeting with CWEL participation (and/or ES participation).

STEP SIX: Assist family in coordinating school meetings and enrollments. Some schools may require orientation attendance, interviews, and so on, and should be coordinated with team while youth is on home passes.

STEP SEVEN (without ES): Verify with the CWEL of new school enrollment and start date.

STEP EIGHT (without ES): Connect the youth team via email with school staff with assistance of the CWEL to monitor progress.

STEP NINE (without ES): Schedule school meeting with the youth team at the school if the situation declines.

OR

STEP SEVEN (with ES): Create an Education Success Plan with the youth and school at a school enrollment meeting once the youth steps down out of facility school.

STEP EIGHT (with ES): Set a school progress meeting with the team and connect all parties via team email.

STEP NINE (with ES): Check attendance weekly and monitor progress.

STEP TEN (with ES): Continue school progress meetings as decided by the youth team.

Special Consideration: Utilization of an ES

While school progress and meetings are outlined as coordinated by ES, if the child welfare caseworker and/or probation officer can take on this role of scheduling school meetings by utilizing the CWEL and points of contact from the action team then the county can proceed without the position. Most roles/responsibilities of agencies/school remain the same with or without an ES as they are all active members in a youth's team and education transition is a team effort.

Parent/Guardian Engagement in Education Transition

Research continually endorses the engagement of families and other supportive adults in major system decisions and processes. Some suggest that engaging parents is the single strongest deterrent from recidivism and delinquent behavior (Brock et al., 2006). In Colorado, the Division of Youth Services involves the family in every step of the process when a youth is detained within the correctional system. Families are crucial in all types of transition and educational planning for youth. With this also comes the understanding that foster care youth may not have a supportive family member. In these circumstances, individual case planning should include an adult mentor and/or at least one supportive member of the youth team who can be a consistent supportive adult through their time in the child welfare and/or justice system. Best practices state that a family should be required to actively involve a family member in all planning for a youth. This is extremely important when special education is identified. Families can work with the team to determine what schools they want to consider and resolve any educational barriers that exist. Parents should visit schools with the youth prior to discharge from a facility and, even, the parent should have all educational records of the youth that the ES obtains throughout the process. This will help empower the parent/guardian to play a critical role in youth transition.

At a minimum, include family in education transition meetings, enrollment meetings, and invite their feedback in improving educational outcomes within systems. Additionally, ways in which professionals speak to families impacts the level of engagement both in schools and systems. It is important to always present information in a way that is understandable without technical terms both in education and agencies. This is particularly important in special education when many special education terms are not understood by families. It is noticed within the 17th Judicial District that, in addition to families, the agency professionals also need further explanation of special education terms. This is an issue that is addressed in this phase under cross-agency training, but the ES should err on the side of caution. Any time school staff utilize technical terms, it is helpful to pause the meeting and check for understanding with the family to ensure they remain engaged in the process. Additionally, the more professionals remain respectful, professional, culturally sensitive, and utilize all forms of contact, the more they can engage families (Brock et al., 2008). Parents/Guardians may also have their own barriers preventing them from actively participating in a youth's education such as time of day, transportation difficulty, work schedules, and/or the need for day care for siblings. All efforts should be made to accommodate the families in these situations such as assisting with transportation, scheduling meetings around work, and encouraging the parent to bring siblings to meetings if necessary. Both schools and agencies alike can consistently be encouraging and supporting parents/families to engage in a youth's education.

New Procedures Data Collection

In this phase, it is discussed how a CWEL and the juvenile justice agency can coordinate for a youth experiencing short detention stays and long-term residential stays. This is a sample procedure that offers a baseline of what is possible in the county in which it is implemented. For the 17th Judicial District, it allows for school districts to know exactly which youth are in the court system in their individual schools. It allows for districts to identify what schools are experiencing the largest population of juvenile justice youth and it triggers educational planning for youth to return to community school. These results are only the beginning in what is possible in terms of education transition for short-term detention stays. The data collected, both positive and negative, could show a need for a direct service staff to work specifically with these youth or prove what current staff are doing is effective. In addition, if the school district administration is not experiencing positive outcomes with the identified youth, they may want to consider working with specific schools to revise policies, review procedures in working with this youth, and possibly revisit school discipline policies. Simply knowing the total number of juvenile justice youth in their school district might change the way they work with the population. The hopeful end result is that every individual youth receives support when stepping down out of detention back into their community school. This can and will look different for every school district with individualized data. Some possible changes include a simple check in with a school administrator to encourage connection to school, remind youth a positive adult supports their academic journey, help youth catch up on work, and/or re-enter into the classroom successfully without feeling behind. All of which contributes to keeping a youth engaged and supported and offset the negativity of education instability.

Establishing New Procedures

Once a plan is designed and new procedures written, the action team must decide how to best implement and sustain it. List all of the involved players who need to know this new procedure and how to introduce the concept. Ask the questions:

- Will this be a large training regime for each agency involved?
- Will this be separate staff meetings to workers or trusting supervisors to distribute information to their teams?
- How will the action team monitor this new procedure and gather information on how it is evolving?

Set a time to meet with staff once a month and then quarterly to elicit feedback until the new procedure is fully integrated. This timeframe will vary by county and plans should be put in motion to write these new procedures in the existing policies and procedures handbook for all agencies involved, including child welfare, probation, pre-trial, and all other relevant parties once the procedure is solidified and all kinks in planning are addressed. These new processes should then be incorporated as a regular component to the cross-agency training initiated by the action team.

Improving Systems Procedures: School Response to Court-Involved Youth

As mentioned throughout this framework, there is not a single system that is solely responsible for improving educational outcomes but rather systems working together not only in procedures and communication but also in how professionals are relating to youth on a daily basis when supporting their educational success. As outside agencies partner with schools to establish a consistent way to identify the court-involved youth in the school, the school can now partner with agencies to keep youth in school once identified. As noted in Advancing School Discipline Reform, "when school discipline practices are aligned with efforts to promote the conditions and opportunities to learn, academic achievement improves" (Colombi & Osher, 2015, p. 3). This process not only involves school district administration setting the tone of positive school responses to court-involved youth but also administrators in their schools creating a paradigm shift from discipline to compassion to keep youth connected to school. This includes the types of discipline put in place and the responses to behaviors in the classroom.

Many others have worked on this particular issue and found a few specific things to be helpful in this effort. In New York, schools found that providing a discipline adviser, more guidance counselors, and substance abuse experts were helpful in the newly created school support centers. It was also helpful to issue "warning cards" instead of criminal tickets (Wall, 2015). Furthermore, juvenile justice referrals from schools fell 75% when schools did not refer a youth for a misdemeanor until the third infraction and after a series of school-based interventions (Siegle et al., 2014). In Ohio, Cleveland school districts integrated an early warning system and created planning centers to utilize in lieu of school suspensions along with other research-based programming. Other school districts see success with local community partnerships, restorative justice programs, family group conferencing, social emotional learning, and positive behavioral interventions. National programming such as Achievement for Latinos Through Academic Success (ALAS) have components that help students learn social and emotional skills, provide positive reinforcement, daily monitoring, and building school to family relationships. While this program is specific to Latino youth, all court-involved youth stand to benefit from such supports. The ALAS program found that to foster achievement, "new bonds needed to be built with at risk Latino students who felt disowned by a school and environment that did not reflect their culture" (Posner, nd, p. 2). This is often necessary for many juvenile justice youth who feel targeted at the school level. As a result of the ALAS efforts, it was found necessary to also collaborate with school administration to change a response to behavior from a discipline measure to additional supports such as tutoring. Another national program, Check and Connect gives youth a two-year mentor that monitors daily attendance, behavior, and grades, often meeting with youth weekly to build relationships and give feedback to youth. All of these are examples of successful programming at the school level that can assist in keeping youth engaged in their schools or re-engage in new schools. In addition, in Pennsylvania, the school district of Philadelphia has a separate transition protocol in determining school placement. This includes attendance by youth of a transition center for up to a month. During the time at the transition center, a transition plan is created including goals and services in returning the youth to regular classrooms. Through this process, recommendations are made by the district for best educational placement and schools learn more about the individual youth in the process. For more information about these and more ways in which schools around the country are initiating or keeping youth engagement, visit the Council for State Governments Justice Center at www. csgjusticecenter.org. While this guide does not expand on a step-by step-guide on to how to improve school culture, it does recommend that the action team put this particular issue on the agenda and partner with a local school that is doing well working with this population in the hope of expanding the work to other schools in the district. Employ the assistance of the school department working with school discipline and expulsions to take a primary role in creating a paradigm shift that promotes responding to court-involved youth in a way that is compassionate and promotes connection to the school instead of dismissing them entirely.

Chapter 15

Cross-Agency Training

Importance

School district professionals benefit from ongoing training around both child welfare and juvenile justice to better collaborate and understand these outside agencies and the resources they provide. The same is true for outside agencies to understand the inner workings of school systems. The Crossover Youth Practice Model (2013) points out that "school partners must be aware of a student's situation at home and the challenges he/she may face ... this involves educating teachers and administrators on what it means for a student to be involved in the child welfare or juvenile justice systems" (p. 9). With regard to the juvenile justice system, research indicates that facilitating regular cross systems training is a "key tool for breaking down systems silos among agencies ... trainings are particularly valuable because some systems are reluctant to work with the juvenile justice system due to the desire to avoid serving high-risk youth" (Siegle et al., 2014, p. 65). It is clear that school professionals are more apt to work with at-risk youth when they are informed and included in team decision making. **Agencies tend to withhold information from school staff based on the assumption that the school will push the youth out of the environment. However, the opposite is true.** When information is withheld, the school professionals are more likely to react by keeping court-involved youth out of the school because they lack the details needed to inform good decisions about educational placement. The more open agency professionals are with schools (while maintaining HIPAA), the more likely the school is to be cooperative in re-engaging and/or maintaining the youth. Cross-agency training is a great way to eliminate this communication barrier by providing face-to-face meetings and fostering new working relationships.

In addition, Griller et al. (2016) indicate, "it is necessary to operate a strong training and professional development program within JJ facilities and agencies" (p. 14). Not only do agencies need to understand schools but agencies working in collaboration with one another need to train each other on valuable information regarding roles, responsibilities, and fundamental framework operating within each agency.

In addition, partnering agencies need consistent training on new educational procedures that the action team implements within their respective agencies to collaborate with one another. An example of this would be the creation of the ES position and training professionals on the purpose of the position and how best to utilize services. The action team first develops brief training for each agency represented on the team, including procedural updates and additions. If possible, within the first year of the action plan, create a goal for the action team to deliver a minimum of one system-to-school or school-to-system training. Within the action plan goal, objectives can include creating a separate training team, holding collaborate meetings to discuss and create a curriculum for at least one cross-agency training.

Identify Existing Successful Training Collaborations

In the beginning stages of forming cross-agency training, be sure to include all existing training provided to agencies and schools. Assessment of training will help determine if the curricula and training frequency are sufficient or require updates. Discuss if these training collaborations are meeting the current need for information and are adequate across systems to fully understand each other's role.

- Is the current training preparing school staff to work with court-involved youth and the demands placed upon them?
- Are schools communicating the best ways to collaborate with school and exchange information?
- Does the systems staff understand how to best partner with schools to keep a youth engaged in school?

These are all questions the action team must ask when looking at existing training frameworks. Finally, ask the question to direct service workers as to what they desire in training topics that would better prepare them to coordinate educational planning. With this information, the action team has a baseline for enhancing current training collaborations and/or building new cross-agency training initiatives.

Next, identify agency training coordinators who can assist in this effort and partner with them to identify existing materials such as presentations, handouts, and curricula. The action team can use these resources to build a specific cross-agency training to meet identified needs. Training does not have to be lengthy. Teams can provide a significant amount of content and include a number of different agencies within one presentation. For example, single training can include the juvenile assessment center with pre-trial supervision, probation, and youth corrections in one presentation as the process flows within juvenile justice from one agency to the next. Along those lines, perhaps mental health, CASA, and child welfare can present together in a separate training. There is certainly a benefit to having all agencies in one training, so the continuum of educational planning can be comprehensive of procedures that occur between child welfare and juvenile justice. Consider the type of venue, timeframe, and refreshments for training. Ask action team members if any can contribute financially for refreshments and/or supplies if necessary.

There are many different ways to coordinate training. Training can be as informal as a meet and greet session that involves a site visit for juvenile probation officers to attend an administrative staff meeting at the local high school. On the other hand, they can be as formal as organizing a half- or full-day session dedicated to cross-agency training of all schools and agencies with designated workshops in each area. Or, perhaps, an online training is developed for staff to view at their leisure and required for new employee training.

Many agencies dedicate staff time to special projects that enhance the lives of clients. There may be staff in the office willing to commit to a cross-agency training project and create material on all the fundamental aspects of a client on probation including a flow chart, roles, responsibilities, and expectations. Perhaps there is already an existent agency presentation that is adaptable to train school staff specifically on roles/responsibilities, court processes, and expectations of probation. For example, a Senate Bill 94 staff member volunteered with the 17th Judicial District probation office and the pre-trial supervision agency to plan a one-hour presentation to Adams County School District building administrators and school resource officers with the potential to conduct this training for any school district upon request. To allocate time for this training, a district administrator can consider coordinating monthly resource meeting time for building administrators that includes time for an information session from outside agencies. In short, it is a good practice to identify the method each agency will use to ensure training supports youth and new processes.

Cross-Agency Training Development

Once the action team has a full picture and understanding of the training needs in the county, cross-agency training will need to be prioritized considering highest training needs and the sustainability to deliver on a regular basis. Ask the following questions to identify specific training logistics:

KEY QUESTIONS: TRAINING DEVELOPMENT

How many people trained per session?

What is the financial cost of creating, providing, and sustaining training?

Are there any financial resources within the action team?

Where will the training be held?

Who is the primary audience?

Will the training be conducted in staff meetings?

Will the training be formal or informal meet and greet sessions?

Should the format be a train the trainer model?

Which training needs to be repeated once a year?

What training format is most sustainable?

What specific topic training do you need?

What is the length of the training and what agencies present together?

What is the role the ES plays that is most helpful in training development?

What members will create curriculum for cross-agency training?

What documents will be implemented and trained on by staff?

Who will commit to regular training to inform outside agencies of the work within the agency and staff role in educational planning as it evolves?

How will training be sustainable long-term?

In order for the action team to establish a training plan for schools and vice versa, agencies will need to coordinate with school district administration to identify time, date, location, and size of training. Utilize the CWEL point of contact to identify a school district administrator to champion these efforts. To plan all logistics and create a training plan, agency representatives must schedule a time to meet with the school administrators who are responsible for coordinating school-level training. At this time, brainstorming sessions between schools and agencies will determine a collaborative training implementation plan. Expect that multiple meetings will be necessary to establish all required logistics and full implementation. Invite the school administrator to be a part of the training team; the administrator can assist in ensuring optimal use of time and that training team meetings are well attended. School district administrators could also consider appointing two representatives, one to provide training to agencies and one to coordinate training within schools. At this point in planning, create a training contact distribution list via email so communications and updates reach all training team members.

Step-by-Step Overview: Cross-Agency Training Development

STEP ONE: Action team identify goal of cross-agency training
STEP TWO: Form a training team and meet separately of action team
STEP THREE: Identify existing training collaborations
STEP FOUR: Meet with agency training coordinators, identify existing materials
STEP FIVE: Schedule school and agency meeting to discuss training needs and logistics
STEP SIX: Develop a training plan to meet action plan goal
STEP SEVEN: Develop or adapt existing curriculum
STEP EIGHT: Conduct training
STEP NINE: Establish regular training schedule and create training contact list

Agency to School Training

Cross-agency training should include but are not limited to agency overview, information sharing, roles and responsibilities, and new procedures around educational planning. Agency training is a good source for introducing the ES and the ES role in providing individual education planning. Cross-agency training absolutely *must* be sustainable and each action team member must commit to making this a priority. Each agency commits to creating a brief presentation about their respective agencies and to train others each year on roles and responsibilities to ensure that collaborations and information sharing continues to grow. At minimum, consider the option for each agency to conduct a brief refresher to the Education Action Team annually. In this capacity, team members can return to respective agencies and share information with all staff. This will also allow for agencies to update the action team on changes and improvements to the agency itself.

Agency to school training provides an opportunity to update contact information, provide regular documentation that can be utilized during educational planning, and ensure all direct service staff are informed on streamlined processes and best practices related to education planning. This training is particularly important for schools that do not know who to contact when a student becomes involved in child welfare and/or juvenile justice. The team should target school building administrators and social workers so the information is funneled down to all school staff. Be advised certain school staff need safety procedural information such as building administrators, while other staff such as counselors and social workers need more information about mental health and direct service partnerships with outside agencies. Thus, knowing the audience is a critical component for effective training.

KEY TRAINING COMPONENTS: AGENCY TO SCHOOL

Information sharing.

Education planning procedures.

Best interest determination procedures.

Needs and expectations of school collaboration with child welfare and juvenile justice.

Roles of agencies: Child welfare, diversion, courts, pre-trial, probation, DYS, DA, CA, GAL, CASA, etc.

Child welfare and juvenile justice introduction to services, procedures, and flow chart of court involvement.

Agency resources.

Expectations of compliance with agencies (probation, pre-adjudication, parole, child welfare).

CWEL role and responsibilities.

ES role and responsibilities.

School to Agency training

For a school district to provide agency training, identify team members willing to commit to the establishment of this training within their agencies. School district staff, possibly the CWEL, in coordination with the ES can develop training. Perhaps the school district administration can identify school staff to provide agency training. Ideally, the school staff selected to facilitate training are familiar with both general and special education procedures. If that is not possible, perhaps a special and a general education staff partner in training to agencies. Agency members in coordination with school staff will have to identify time, location, size, and frequency of training provided. Typically, agencies have a training coordinator within their agencies. Establish a partnership with any existent training coordinators. Utilize coordinator expertise to establish either large multi-agency training or smaller individual agency training. This guide does not seek to dictate this development; only the action team knows what type of training will suit individual needs and which are sustainable.

KEY TRAINING COMPONENTS: SCHOOL TO AGENCY

Introduction to general, special education, RtI, 504.

Suspension and expulsion discipline policies.

Point of contact for specific education needs.

Alternative school options.

Need and expectations of agency collaboration and involvement.

Role in best interest determinations.

Special education specific details as it relates to discipline, qualification, evaluations, and services.

Transportation procedures.

Cross-Agency Training:
Educational Direct Service

The ES providing direct service to court-involved youth (phase 3) will work to create his/her own training for agencies and schools to introduce a new way of providing direct service educational planning. Ideally, this training introduces the position, further clarifies involvement, point of contact utilization, resources, and educational planning services specific to this role. Make sure to include notification/referral procedures and points of contact. The action team may see it beneficial to incorporate this role into the school cross-agency training or it could become separate training to agencies and schools. Phase 3 describes this position in detail and provides information that can be expanded upon to specify the ES position to the county in which it is implemented.

Chapter 16

Formal Training

Importance of Formal Training

Identify Need

Training is important in understanding all dynamics existing in working with individual youth. According to Seigle et al. (2014):

> Young people are not mini-adults. Their families, peers, schools and communities have a significant influence on their beliefs and actions. They engage in risky behaviors, fail to account for the long-term consequences of their decisions, and are relatively insensitive to degrees of punishment. They also struggle to regulate their impulses and emotions. A growing body of research confirms that these differences are developmental – the result of biological and neurological conditions unique to adolescence – and that ignoring these distinct aspects of adolescent development can undermine the potential positive impact of system interventions and even do more harm than good.
>
> (p. 41)

Not all agencies and schools have a working knowledge of child and adolescent development across the spectrum as it may not have been a part of their formal education. Most are only trained in their respective areas of practice and how that relates to a youth. For example, a juvenile probation officer may be educated in the criminal justice proceedings but may not understand how trauma may be impacting a youth's ability to be compliant. There is always a need for professional development due to ever changing best practice and new research in the field. NDTAC (2011) suggests, "professional development opportunities can be organized to increases awareness of programs and practices, which should increase communication, cooperation, and coordination" (p. 17). When the action team identified the gaps in service during phase I, areas of need for formal training were most likely evident. Some targeted service areas in Colorado, specific to House Bill 1451 efforts, might already be offering training opportunities that the team can utilize for their respective agencies. Perhaps, it is clear that schools need more training on the impact of trauma in the classroom. Perhaps court officials and probation officers need training on adolescent development. Child welfare may have foster parents in need of a formal training on special education and/or educational planning for foster youth. During the information collection phase, action teams gathered information on training topics staff identified as a need. This is the time to meet that need.

Suggestions for Formal Training

The National Center for Mental Health and Juvenile Justice (NCMHJJ) saw a need to develop training for juvenile justice about all adolescent development, modality, and treatment. This training ensures that professionals are trained on a youth's mental health services and needs, thus improving collaboration on behavioral health outcomes.

Colorado Education Initiative (a Colorado Department of Education partner organization) offers social and emotional training to schools looking to improve the social emotional component of their school culture. Training around adolescent and child development is also crucial in understanding factors that impact court-involved youth in the classroom.

Furthermore, the Colorado Department of Education has a dropout/prevention program that oversees the utilization of all CWELs in the state. The coordinator for this initiative may be able to speak to respective agencies about laws regulating the CWEL position in Colorado. Look within the state to see what initiatives exist within the state education department.

Finally, a topic that has gained a lot of buzz in the last few years is related to trauma-informed care, as it provides a fundamental understanding of the mental state of many court-involved youth. Some even speculate that a youth's stay in detention causes a traumatic response. If this is true, most, if not all, juvenile delinquents have experienced some type of trauma in their lifetime. Youth in the child welfare system often experience traumatic events inside their home of origin in addition to trauma related to being removed from their parents and placed in foster care. Professionals cannot begin to speculate the trauma that could ensue beyond that initial entrance into the child welfare system.

There are many trauma-informed care initiatives throughout the state. However, it appears that the trauma training reaches more to outside agencies than to school staff. Through the action team, utilize outside agency resources to determine what trauma training is happening across the county and build on that resource. As mentioned previously, staff meetings within agencies and schools are a great time to coordinate informal and even formal training. Most agencies and schools are required to provide professional development and this is an opportunity to collaborate.

Parent/Guardian and Foster Parent Training

Within the training team, identify the training currently conducted with the parent and compile a list of foster and biological parent training resources in the community. Child welfare agencies maintain a training department that is most likely providing training to foster parents. It behooves the training team and/or the ES to meet with the departmental staff to discuss what education training parents already receive and what the team and/or ES may add to this training. Perhaps it is helpful for the ES to contribute a portion of education training to already existing parent and/or foster parent training, or work with the department to create new specific educational planning training. Ensure that if someone from the action team and/or the ES does participate in this training that he/she is a regular member of the team and continues to contribute up-to-date information to foster and biological parents.

It is important to note, parents may express a need for training specifically in special education, as this system is detailed and confusing at times. However, not every parent will need this information. Within the county, identify and compile a list of local special education agencies promoting advocacy and education. These agencies may offer parent training and individual case advocacy. A bit of outreach to these agencies may find that they are willing to present to professionals working with youth in special education. For example, the Arc of Adams County already offers parent training. The 17th JD Education Advocate first attended parent training and later partnered with an Arc advocate to train foster parents, juvenile justice, child welfare, and juvenile justice parents with one day and evening training sessions. Ensure that the training, if initiated, is sustainable long-term. At a minimum, partner with these agencies to refer youth who need more intensive special education advocacy than what an ES might be able to provide.

Training Sustainability

Cross-agency training will continue to be an important part of sustaining the improved coordination of educational planning. Part of this process is ongoing training to staff on new procedures and accounting for staff turnover. The action team should designate staff, at minimum, from the three most involved agencies: school, probation, and child welfare, to address training needs for educational planning on a yearly basis. Ensuring that all staff are informed on the need for educational planning and the proper channels for such planning is crucial. One action team member should commit to maintaining a regular contact list. The other team members identified will meet yearly to discuss the needs for cross-agency training based on staff turnover, the adherence to educational planning, and the efficiency of new processes. Cross-agency training is half the battle in ensuring that agency and school staff have a shared understanding of their roles on a youth team.

Tips from the Field: Examples of Formal Training Collaborations

Joel Hendershott conducts workshops and training on his book "Healing the Wounded Student" and is accessible via the website at www.hope4thewounded.org/books-and-more.

The Massachusetts Advocates for Children produced a book "Helping Traumatized Children Learn." This organization offers training and copies of their books can be ordered online and are helpful for teachers, caseworkers, and any direct service working with court-involved youth (http://massadvocates.org/publications/).

Some states have adopted formal mental health training for probation officers. Other juvenile justice agencies have adopted the Effective Practices in Community Supervision (EPICS) model to enhance supervision practices and encourage professionals to target youth risk factors utilizing case planning, build positive relationships with the youth and give positive reinforcements (Seigle et al., 2014).

In other states, child welfare departments trained probation officers in the Functional Family Therapy (FFT) design and adapted this model to create Functional Family Probation (FFP). "FFP probation officers maintain traditional probation functions, but have reduced caseloads and work in a family's home using FFT techniques to promote youth and family behavior change" (Siegle et al., 2014 p. 45).

"KISR in school rule today and tomorrow" (2015) mentioned how Legal Aid attorneys in Cincinnati, OH, conduct numerous training courses on education law and school issues. Legal Aid attorneys represent youth on issues related to enrollment, school discipline, and special education.

Whatever the action team decides, ensure that it is replicable and can be repeated regularly to ensure new staff are always trained on the same procedures to ensure consistency.

Phase 3

Individual Interventions

Chapter 17

Phase 3 Introduction and Importance

The direct service procedures within phase 3 are for both education staff (ES) working toward educational planning and for caseworkers/individuals working on youth cases. Procedures describe ways in which child welfare and juvenile justice staff can address accountability in school and monitor education needs and performance consistently. Each person within the team of individuals working with youth to improve educational outcomes has a role that is essential to the bigger systems-level work.

This phase describes the recommended direct service procedures for all foster care, school age, crossover, and juvenile justice youth. Roles may look different depending on the agencies involved in the case, but the underpinning goal of working collectively to support educational needs remains the same. The action team will utilize the example procedures for direct service and adapt them to fit the specific needs of the ES. Overall, the direct service procedures address common issues with system accountability and educational progress monitoring. Direct service procedures are also designed to address the individual academic needs of court-involved youth.

It is well studied and documented that child welfare youth who have unattended learning and emotional development deficits often present with behavioral issues in the classroom, which tends to shift focus away from their academic performance (Finkelstein et al., 2002). With this understanding, it is the duty of the direct service providers to identify deficits upon entrance into the child welfare system to prevent school disengagement and/or future juvenile justice involvement. Since developmental and learning deficits are not always apparent at the beginning of a case, academic performance must be monitored consistently as a preventative measure. It is worth noting, however, that identifying deficits and monitoring academic performance upon case initiation is new, and these preventative measures are a paradigm shift from the education service procedures that currently exist, if any exist at all. As such, initial pushback from direct service staff can be anticipated, as they may not view education as a priority among all other treatment concerns. It is important to remain insistent upon addressing education immediately when opening child welfare and juvenile justice cases. Take it from California where it is known that the education liaison direct service model, which operationalized academic monitoring at case inception, was effective in "increasing the level of knowledge of social workers about educational procedures and programs for supporting the educational needs of foster youth ... increasing social workers' level of participating in the educational process of children on their caseloads ... increasing the social workers documentation of up-to-date education information including in the children's case files, and ... improving the math and reading achievement test scores of children" (Leone & Weinberg, 2012, p. 43).

In the special report, *Don't Call Them Dropouts,* Gomperts (2014) indicated that young people who leave high school before graduating display resilience due to difficult circumstances in childhood. However, in order to re-engage, youth require more than just internal academic grit. Moreover, Gomperts (2014) reports, "consistent with the principles of positive youth development, young people began to thrive academically, socially, and emotionally when they were able to connect to individuals and institutions that support them" (p. 5). Youth need to feel support and connection. The more they are connected, the less they act out (Macaluso, 2015). Overall, "young people require consistent support from people and places that combine caring connections with the capacity to help them navigate around obstacles" (Gomperts, 2014, p. 3). However, despite these necessary supports, professionals still experience significant barriers re-engaging youth in school. In Cook County, officials found that "despite court orders requiring that they attend school, youth were regularly denied reentry into their home school" (Leone & Weinberg, 2012, p. 18). Further recognizing that while the individual interventions are important, the county and systems collaboration is of equal importance to create and sustain phase 3 so youth engagement can be successful.

In line with evidence-based practice, phase 3 provides guidance on nurturing youth to foster positive connections with school staff, understanding barriers, identifying academic needs, and surrounding youth with a culture that is supportive of individual academic goals. With this model, teams are both engaging the youth to graduate and building a foundation for success in the future.

Especially important within the juvenile justice field, schools and professionals must work to pave an easier way for returning to education verses allowing an easy exit. In reviewing the literature, Lewis (2015) noted, "with strained resources, large classes, and the placement of special needs children in mainstream classrooms, teachers feel poorly equipped to manage the kids who are especially challenging and uncooperative" (p. 2). When schools easily dismiss youth for discipline or attendance without much attempt to understand the root cause of such behaviors, youth are further alienated from an already limited source of safe community of supports that can and are willing to help with their success. To this end, an ES can do what school staff may not have time for in the larger school settings. The ES can engage youth in conversations that reaches to the core issues and identifies what the youth feels he/she needs most to be successful in school. The ES is well positioned to nurture the youth in building a path to success while also identifying the underlying internal barriers that may require additional interventions. The ES can then build a team around individualized academic success that is grounded in communication and a common goal of support rather than school dismissal. This youth team should typically include but is not limited to caseworkers, probation officers, pre-trial officers, school contact, therapist, GAL, and CASA. At the core of this communication, professionals must provide a safe space for youth to participate in the choices that impact their academic futures.

In addition to systems collaboration and direct service supports, youth must be encouraged to choose their own path in order to foster full engagement. Professionals cannot force a path that a youth does not feel is personally relevant to the intentions set for his/her life. Youth must create their own goals and those goals must not be guided in any way by others. Professionals must keep in mind that "attributes that protect students from making poor academic decisions can only be understood from the aspect of the student's private logic" (Lemon & Watson, 2011, pp. 17–22). In other words, adults must understand the foundational beliefs a youth has about him/her self and others in order to understand how to help. Due to life circumstance, youth in the system often display strengths including, among many others, grit, ability to thrive despite odds, and creative problem-solving skills. Professionals must build upon these strengths constructively by relating them to education. The youth team can assist to nurture these traits to support the youth in achieving his/her personal positive education goals. A study reported in 2014 to further understand foster care youth experiences and perspectives on education by Levy et al. (2014) found that youth expressed the need for internal determination and motivation to succeed in school despite barriers. Youth reported a realization that they had to make the decision internally before they would be successful. Research finds that "a youth who is at risk needs to incorporate high school completion into personal value system and to bridge individual meaning, making processes in relation to life, goals, self and others with high school graduation" (Lemon & Watson, 2011, pp. 17–22). Phillips (2011) said it well, "If we do not ask students about their perceptions and experiences with education, and if we do not listen to their answers, then we run the risk of creating experiences that they feel are unimportant ... ignoring what they think about learning, we take away their ownership, agency, and interest in education" (p. 8). Though not shocking, literature also indicates that negativity within youth environments, relationships, and school climates also hinder youth learning and could have potentially permanent effects. According to Phillips (2011), "students are more likely to engage positively in school when they feel that their ideas have been listened to and validated." (p. 2). When their voice is ignored, youth will disengage even if only to their own detriment. In order to contribute to youth success, systems and the ES must incorporate the positive elements into their respective environments to improve educational outcomes and actively listen to the desires of youth for their own future. If professionals are disingenuous or fragmented in the approach to educational planning, they will lose youth trust in their intentions. Always consider the youth as an equal partner of the team.

This final phase, phase 3, is aligned with and covers goals five and six of the *Blueprints for Change: Educational Success for Youth in Foster Care* (2014). These goals aim to implement preventative supports to avoid dropout, truancy, and disciplinary actions, as well as empowering youth to advocate for their educational pursuits through engagement in all aspects of education and educational planning. *Blueprints for Change* specifically suggested that "youth are entitled to have a knowledgeable and trained education advocate who reinforces the value of the youth's investment in education and helps the youth plan" (p. 2). Furthermore, the *Blueprints for Change: Educational Success for Youth in Juvenile Justice* (2016) was recently released and reinforces a few other themes presented in this guide—youth should remain in the home or community school after becoming involved in the justice system involvement; plans for the youth should include and be informed by the youth; and re-entry planning and supports are imperative for all school/justice transitions and placements. In short, the goals outlined in each of the *Blueprints for Change* books serve as a call to action, and phase 3 of this guide provides the framework and tools for the action.

Phase 3 is primed for success when the interventions from phases 1 and 2 are in place. The ES is able to provide individualized educational planning services because the standards for communication about each case are established and systems are communicating with consistency. Therefore, the ability for the ES to provide individualized services is directly related to the effectiveness of systems communication. For systems that fail to adopt standards of notification, the unnecessary and numerous efforts to catch up on overlooked cases and coordinate systems around each case will be the responsibility of the ES at the cost of the direct service that could otherwise be provided.

Phase 3 recommendations rely on the systems procedures outlined in phase 2. Ideally, an ES is notified of the case at initial entry. Research repeatedly recommends that transition and educational planning should start early to ensure that all entities involved are collaborating for a successful transition out of the system so the notification at time of entry allows for services to start immediately. In addition, the latest research reported from The National Evaluation and Technical Assistance Center supports that "receiving and managing a youth's education records should be the responsibility of one staff person" (Clark et al., 2016 p. 14). This step will minimize any confusion of roles and keeps education consistent throughout youth involvement in the system. While this person will maintain all education records and planning, he/she also encourages the parent/guardian to maintain an educational file as well. Everything that the direct service staff has should also be reflected in the parent/guardian file. Ideally, systems involvement will not be long-term, so it is important to engage the parent/guardian at every level of planning. By the close of the case, the parent should be the biggest education advocate for the youth and initiating all education meetings, decisions, and support.

Phase 3 Key Terms

Youth team: All professionals and at least one member of school staff who are assigned to an individual youth case. A typical youth team is inclusive of caseworker, probation officer, pre-trial supervisor, diversion officer, case manager, GAL, CASA, SRO, and therapist.

School enrollment meeting: School enrollment meetings refer to an interview for enrollment in a new school or a discussion aimed to help a youth engage with a new school.

School progress meetings: School progress meetings are scheduled with the youth team and family for monitoring any academic assistance provisions that are in place for the youth.

Education Success Plan: Plan developed by the youth, youth team, and other school/system stakeholders that indicate how the youth will re-engage in the school environment. The education success plan is written during a school progress or enrollment meeting.

Education Intake Form: An information collection tool for assessing academic performance. The form offers a standardized method for establishing a baseline for progress and can be assessed based on youth progress to goals, trauma, behavior, and current academic standing.

Education Passport Form: The education passport is a contact summary and checklist of information contained in an educational file—it is essentially a cover page of information relevant to school enrollment and/or transition. The education passport indicates the biological parent, caseworker, probation officer, previous schools, and checkboxes for identifying the documents within the file. This form is utilized when a youth is enrolling in a new school and/or during transition times. This form should be updated and sent to each new school in order to reflect all previous school placements.

Section 504 Plan: A 504 plan contains the approved classroom accommodation(s) that must be made for youth who have a documented impairment (physical or otherwise). A school Section 504 coordinator can hold a meeting to determine Section 504 eligibility. If a youth does not qualify for an Individualized Education Plan under special education or the impairment does not require a special education evaluation certain accommodations can be easily met with a 504 plan.

Seat hours: Seat hours indicate the amount of academic time youth have spent in a classroom. Academic seat hours accumulate to earned credits. For example, in Colorado 30 seat hours are the equivalent of a quarter credit, 60 seat hours are the equivalent of a half credit, and 120 seat hours are one full credit hour toward the core academics for which the seat hour reports were issued. Detention centers and facilities issue seat hour reports in transcripts in Colorado. This may vary state to state depending on the school district under which a detention or residential center falls.

Chapter 18

Building Academic Success

According to the Philliber Research Associates (2013), self-efficacy is said to be one of the greatest predictors of perseverance among youth in school. Youth can build self-efficacy when adults model certain academic skills, such as goal setting and responding positively to feedback, and youth then follow suit by also setting goals and practicing a positive response to academic feedback. Similar to teaching student skills, workers who understand a task, are shown a task, and are provided training and feedback on the task, also then perform positively and build self-efficacy.

With regard to individual characteristics, "passion and purpose, grit and growth and identity and community" (Snipes et al., 2012, p. 7) are all associated with successful educational outcomes. More specifically, grit is thought to be an internal motivation, attitude, and/or determination maintained over time despite failures. Some in this field argue that court-involved youth already have grit and passion fundamentally built into their personality as they have possibly survived a range of traumatic experiences at an early age. Professionals must help youth take their personal grit and passion and apply it to academics and future aspirations for which they are passionate in pursuing.

Another area for consideration in working with this client population is self-regulation. Youth who display healthy characteristics in dealing with stress, managing impulses, overcoming problems, emotional expression, and successfully creating and monitoring own goals show higher educational outcomes. However, court-involved youth who have experienced significant trauma in their history often have trouble with many of these behaviors within self-management, making classroom environments difficult at times. Unfortunately, exposure to juvenile justice systems such as arrest, court, and detention may further youth traumatic experiences. Some speculate this can impact school performance and behavior as well (Ford et al., 2007). Both child welfare youth and juvenile justice youth are known to have deficits both academically and emotionally. As a result, educators, advocates, and direct staff working with youth must be mindful that court-involved youth may need assistance with learning social emotional skills specifically to help promote academic success. It is well known that an earlier intervention beginning in childhood is best. If schools and agencies can provide social-emotional skill building early in childhood, the risk of systems involvement decreases (Rankin & Gonsoulin, 2014). Academic skills are not retained if youth cannot self-regulate in the classroom. Colorado Education Initiative (2014), recognizing this important component, created the Social Emotional Framework for all general education students. Literature supporting implementing social emotional learning in schools can be found in numerous studies including one of 213 school-based programming across the country providing youth a social emotional specific program from kindergarten to high school. It was found that youth showed marked improvements in academic performance due to a significant increase in social emotional competency, attitude, and behavior compared with the control group (Durlak, et al. 2011). Recommendations for social emotional programming specific to juvenile justice are noted by many organizations including the National Evaluation and Technical Assistance Center for the Education of Neglected or Delinquent Children and Youth (NDTAC).

Finally, the University of Chicago, through a review of research in 2012, outlined four main academic mindsets that are necessary for a youth to succeed academically:

I belong to this academic community;
I can succeed at this;
My ability and competence grow with my efforts, and
This work has value for me.

(Farrington et al., 2012, p 28)

Once a direct service staff has experience in the field, it is easy to identify in a youth which academic mindset he/she specifically needs to build in order to re-engage in academics. According to Snipes et al. (2012), the reason behind focusing on, "academic mindsets is that student's attitudes, beliefs, and dispositions affect the quality, duration, and intensity with which students engage in critical academic behaviors and deploy learning strategies that, in turn, can powerfully affect student learning and academic outcomes" (p. 6). In regard to feeling a sense of belonging, research shows that relationship building is more important in high schoolers than elementary students, suggesting that connecting to an academic community is extremely important to many adolescent court-involved youth. Literature supports the use of mentors as a positive support in building community relationships as well (Skyles et al., 2007). It has been found that including at least one caring adult can make the difference in academic progress. Teachers can potentially be a support in this realm as well by engaging youth in conversations about progress or lack thereof, thus showing their level of interest and genuine concern for youth (Rosenkranz et al., 2014). Disengaged youth report often not feeling validated, heard, or cared for by their teachers. As a result, professionals must pay close attention to the relationships built with youth knowing that "value placed on these relationships can lead young people toward or away from school" (Gomperts, 2014, p. 12) and it is known that juvenile justice youth face negative odds of graduation. In the last ten years, the 17th Judicial District Education Advocate indicates the mindsets that lack the most with 17th Judicial District clients are "belonging to the academic community" and "this work has value for me." This is indicative of the research suggesting the need for more attachment to school community, personally important curriculum, caring adult connections, and more personal identification of academic goals. The literature finds that, "students who have a growth mindset, who feel a sense of identify and belonging to a school community and who experience learning as meaningful and valuable are more likely...to sustain positive academic behaviors" (Snipes et al., 2012 p. 8). In the article, *A Case for School Connectedness* (2005), it is mentioned that youth who stay connected to school experience less, "disruptive behavior, school violence, substance use" (p. 3). This builds a case that academic engagement can possibly deter delinquent behavior entirely or at minimum avoid further systems involvement. While all of these supports may not be available in every school, one can be creative in building in some of these components in communities and within schools. In the appendices, there are case plan and education intake documents that include identifying the academic mindset that is most relevant to individual youth.

For example, a youth in Adams County desperately wanted to return to his home high school despite being over age and under credit. The youth was actively recovering from drug addiction and juvenile justice involvement. The ES and the Dean met with the youth and put in a very specific schedule of classes and connected the youth with school event planning as he had dreams of pursuing a career as a DJ. He was able to help with coordination of pep rallies and mixed the music for the events. He became connected with his academic community and showed great success in mixing music, positive peer connections, and academic progress.

Additionally, it is important for education planning when working with court-involved youth to include special education staff if youth are deemed eligible for special education. It is evident that youth with any type of special education disability are more vulnerable to juvenile justice involvement. The National Longitudinal Transition Study 2 (2006) found around 63% of youth in a national sample of more than 11,000 students in 7th grade or higher, who identified emotional disabilities and were receiving special education services during 2000–2001, experienced more suspensions and expulsions in a school year than their general education peers. This can certainly lead to juvenile justice involvement when a youth is out of school or causing trouble in schools. Additionally, youth with special education needs can be particularly difficult to work with for those not exposed to this population often, as well as for those professionals that are (Larson & Turner, 2002). Any youth with a learning disability might have trouble understanding court proceedings, and professionals may find it challenging to present information in a way that a youth can understand. Often, the Education Advocate in the 17th Judicial District will direct professionals by way of the Individualized Education Plan to determine how best to work with youth and effectively explain court documents, rules, and proceedings. It is possible that a youth was deemed eligible for special education prior to court involvement or systems may deem a special education evaluation necessary when a youth enters into the system for either learning or emotional disabilities. It is important for ES staff to have training on the law and language in the special education field to better identify, advocate, and plan for youth. This also allows for the proper school staff to immediately get involved in educational planning. Youth have access to many different accommodations and individualized learning under the umbrella of special education. With the proper notifications and cross-agency training in place from phases 1 and 2, a school has the potential to notify staff that youth are receiving special education, connect the agency with the school case manager for youth, and provide accordingly appropriate educational planning services and explanations on how to work best with youth in the court system. In addition, the emergence of new mental health diagnosis combined with academic difficulties can lead to a conversation with school staff about the need for a special education evaluation that may have not been considered until systems involvement. More information on incorporating special education school staff in phase 3 is detailed below.

Educational Intake Purpose

While some recommend assessments on all impacted areas such as mental, emotional, behavioral, and disabilities present at the time the youth is brought into a detention facility or placed out of home, this guide goes a step further by recommending the completion of an initial educational intake at the beginning of every case for which the ES receives notice. As an ES working directly with youth on remaining in the community schools or understanding academic needs within facilities, it is necessary to know the academic level in which the youth is operating to establish a baseline for progress monitoring to show improvement. In addition, either systems entry experience, removal from home by child welfare, or being arrested can have quite an impact on a youth's mental health. As a result, questions around trauma impacting academics are also included. Youth may struggle in school long before systems involvement; in which case, education intake at the time of systems entry is crucial in achieving long-term academic success. In addition, if the youth eventually moves to a new school or home, the ES already has baseline information and can quickly transition a youth into a new school with all the relevant documentation.

As noted by the 17th Judicial District Education Advocate, a youth can enter into the juvenile justice system with a behavioral record from home school with details of behavioral incidents beginning in elementary school that have disrupted consistent attendance. Yet, the youth was not identified for special education evaluation or as needing any behavioral modifications within the classroom. To that end, this framework establishes an immediate response to this issue. The ES will immediately have records and can then compare with not only youth reported answers within the intake but an interview with the parent and school as well. The ES can then move forward with a school meeting and evaluating what steps are necessary to determine if mental health is impeding the ability to maintain and learn in the classroom. This may entail Response to Intervention (RtI) remedial classes, the writing of a 504 plan, or a full SPED evaluation.

To fully support youth academically and individualize each educational plan, the action team needs to implement an educational intake form at the direct service level conducted either by an ES or the caseworker/supervising agency. For the purposes of this guide, an educational intake form was created as a baseline for agency personalization. This form covers demographics, school, academic strengths and weaknesses, motivational levels, and questions related to trauma. Further examples of educational intakes exist in Washington, California, and possibly others by the time this guide is in print.

Trauma and Academic-Related Research

In the past few years, the impact of trauma on youth has surfaced as an important issue that is often overlooked in the field and misdiagnosed as a mental health condition. A study out of Cook County cited that 92.5% of youth surveyed had at least one trauma, 84% with more than one trauma, and 56% with six or more traumatic events (Office of Juvenile Justice Delinquency & Prevention, 2014). As an ES, it is important to distinguish between triggered trauma behaviors and a true underlying mental health condition. It is important to illicit feedback from the youth's education team to compare current functioning and diagnosis to past academic history. Helping Traumatized Children Learn (2013) cites academic skill deficits as related to Post-Traumatic Stress Disorder (PTSD) and possibly co-morbid mental health disorders and those are;

> Language and Communication Skills;
> Learning and retrieving new verbal information;
> Social and emotional communication;
> Problem solving and analysis;
> Organizing Narrative Materials;
> Cause-and-Effect Relationships;
> Taking another's Perspective;
> Attentiveness to Classroom Tasks;
> Regulating Emotions;
> Executive Functions;
> Engaging in Curriculum.

(Cole et al., pp. 22–32)

Many PTSD symptoms and behavioral problems originate from the same reason as academic struggles—the inability to process social cues and to convey feelings in an appropriate manner. Often, ADHD and PTSD/trauma can coexist or be misdiagnosed. Behaviors such as reactivity and impulsivity, aggression, defiance, withdrawal, or striving to perfectionism can all be related to trauma experiences or PTSD. Furthermore, the same behaviors manifesting from trauma are also evident in learning disability special education youth as well. The result of which is often due to a frustration in unsuccessful attempts at understanding academic material. Professionals will see additional difficulty in problem solving, self-control, impulsivity, emotional regulation, and anger (Larson & Turner, 2002). It is crucial to distinguish between trauma and emotional or learning disabilities by either conducting psychological and/or special education evaluations. All too often, youth are misdiagnosed with mental health conditions or disabilities that do not exactly fit the individual. It is the duty of the professionals involved to seek more information if the youth continues to struggle despite modified academic settings and interventions. As a result of the established partnership from phase 1 of this guide, professionals and school staff can now partner closely and share information on each case to identify exactly what a youth needs to academically succeed.

Importance of Monitoring Progress

Once a youth has the initial school planning meeting, it is the objective of the ES and the educational team to monitor youth progress. Numerous studies support a continual progress monitoring of a youth once re-engaged in school. NDTAC (2016) identifies this in its *Stage 1: Entry into the Juvenile Justice System* and supports having regular school progress meetings where agency representatives should be involved to streamline services and information pertinent to youth success. The ES will not only organize and facilitate school progress meetings but also track attendance, behavior, and grades weekly and send to all members of the team working with the youth. If the county does not have an ES, it is the responsibility of the caseworker or probation officer to conduct these meetings for at least the first three months after the initial school meeting. Make sure to clarify within the agency of the roles of who will take the lead on this when initially creating and implementing educational procedures to eliminate any and all confusion.

The benefit of having an ES is profound on a youth's progress. The ES is able to obtain specific details about a youth's academics that are typically not collected during a youth's time in the system. The ES will see if the youth begins to decline academically at any point and can intervene immediately. Often, when there is not an ES to monitor a case, a youth may go weeks not attending school without professionals noticing the absences. In addition, multiple school transitions lead to large time lapses in instructional time. For example, a youth moving from one math class to another in a different school district may miss learning certain fundamental math skills such as fractions, decimals, and so on, of which professionals are not aware. The more a youth moves schools, the more the academic deficit is apparent. It often goes unnoticed that a youth can be learning a particular skill in one class and move to the next school where that content was already reviewed. If the youth has not learned this content entirely, a deficit can quickly develop. Without an adult consistently monitoring this issue, youth can easily fall through the cracks of the education system while deficits continue to grow. The current education system is not designed to accommodate this issue. This results in high school age foster and juvenile youth who have not moved beyond an elementary grade level in basic reading and math skills. Such is the downside of large child welfare and probation officer caseloads. If an ES is not monitoring progress, systems will not know if these grade levels increase due to ES involvement on individual cases.

Chapter 19

Special Considerations

Crossover Youth

Many youth are involved with both the child welfare and juvenile justice systems. It will depend on which system the youth was first involved in as to how the ES becomes involved in the case. If the youth is in foster care and incurs criminal charges, the ES should already have a file of educational records and intake on the youth. If the youth is initially brought into the system via criminal charges, the ES receives notification from a juvenile justice agency. Hopefully, if the action team is successful in maintaining the education of foster youth more consistently, and they are changing schools less often, the crossover rate in the county will be impacted as youth are initially experiencing a decrease in disengagement from school. If the action team implements the ES position for child welfare and juvenile justice individually, the action team must clarify who will take the lead on what case so as to not duplicate services. The action team will also have to write into procedures the ways in which these two positions will best collaborate on cases.

These youth often require more attention to education as not only are they going between foster homes but may also have time in detention and/or residential facilities including a possible stay in a division of youth corrections if the youth cannot be maintained in the community. Ensure that if a crossover youth enters detention facilities, the ES obtains educational transcripts upon release. It is important to note in Colorado and perhaps other states, detention center education staff are employed by the local school district in which the detention center is located. While all residential facilities maintain data on one central Colorado facilities database, detention centers are not a part of this database. As a result, detention centers issue transcripts detailing academic seat hours that can be applied to a youth transcript in the next school. The ES will need to undertake a new transcript request each time a youth leaves detention and share it with the school of enrollment. Pay particular attention to behavioral records of crossover youth and rule out any underlying issues that may be inhibiting academic success, particularly where child welfare was involved first at a younger age not related to delinquency. The youth may have academic deficits as a result of moving schools or trauma impact related to involvement in the foster care system. Ensure that the foster parent and/or biological parent is always notified and encouraged to participate (if parental rights are intact) in any educational planning.

Juvenile Correctional Youth

In regards to youth who were committed to juvenile corrections, Synder (2004) in *An Empirical Portrait of the Youth Reentry Population* reported, "these youth are arguably at greater risk of failure than any group served by the juvenile justice system and are likely to be classified as failures of the juvenile justice system if their behaviors do not improve following release from custody" (p. 54). If the ES has worked with these youth prior to commitment, it might behoove the corrections youth team to initiate collaboration with the ES to coordinate transition. In the 17th Judicial District, the Education Advocate has conducted a training to state parole officers operating in the 17th Judicial District on the transition procedures and documents used in the field for Education Advocate clients to keep transitions with schools similar and expectations consistent. There are times where youth will come back into the same community after a correctional commitment. The ES should establish a working relationship with state parole officers working within the county to ensure that he/she is notified of a youth transitioning back into a community school so as to help coordinate services and comply with transition procedures established in the county. State Corrections Departments have their own parole officers who work to create transition plans after long-term residential confinement and the procedure by which youth are transitioned is a procedure that spans across the entire state. In that sense, parole officers may not be as familiar with every differing county level procedure and resource. Oftentimes, singular schools often do not know the difference between parole, probation or pre-trial and assume all are operating with the similar procedures. As a result, it behooves systems to ensure those procedures are similar for the sake of consistency and a standard of practice across all levels. It may be that there is a past relationship already established between ES and youth prior to commitment. Utilize this positive relationship as a stepping stone to re-engagement in community schools. In recent years, transition planning for correctional youth has received much attention. Adding the ES assistance in collaborating pre-commitment transition planning to corrections post-commitment transition planning simply strengthens the practice. In phase 2, the transition procedures were solidified and now the action team should establish how the ES will interface with corrections specifically. An example of this procedure would include situations where the parole officer assists in creating the transition plan for a youth, which includes going back to a community school to finish a high school diploma. The parole officer contacts the ES to connect to the home community school for enrollment procedures. The ES explains the enrollment process to the parole officer and assists in contacting the school principal for an enrollment meeting. This youth may be one the ES worked with before commitment, so the youth then immediately recognizes the ES as a support in the community. The professionals working with recently released youth are now all connected to specific community supports and school simply works within the same transition procedures already established, such as trusting that the ES will always be the initial point of contact.

Special Education

National statistics show that anywhere from 30% to 60% of youth have disabilities in the juvenile justice system. Research cites that youth with a learning disability are two times more likely to commit a crime than non-disabled peers (Brier, 1989; Synder, 2004). Youth with disabilities who are eligible for special education and related services have a right to free appropriate public education (FAPE) from their home school district. Youth suspected to have either an emotional or learning disability possibly impeding his/her ability to learn in the general education classroom should be considered for a special education evaluation. The youth team must also take into account the impact of school missed and past trauma as well when considering a full evaluation.

Often, youth involved in the child welfare or juvenile justice have a disability that has been either misdiagnosed or has gone unnoticed due to dependency and neglect. There are a variety of reasons why a youth may have not yet been identified for special education. It is the responsibility of the youth's education team and the ES to determine if the special education the youth is currently receiving is adequately meeting the needs of the youth, or if a youth is not identified, if a special education evaluation is warranted.

Colorado has implemented the Response to Intervention (RtI) program that is defined as "a multi-tier approach to the early identification and support of students with learning and behavior needs" (Gorski, 2018, p. 1). RtI is a general education program and if a youth is to be evaluated for special education, the youth will move through the RtI process of interventions either before or during the special education evaluation. It is not mandatory that a youth go through the entire RtI process *prior* to a special education evaluation as some might assume. While that process is preferred, it is not always possible with court-involved youth. The youth may come into a new school and the need for a special education evaluation is immediate so RtI is implemented while the evaluation is in process. RtI can also benefit many general education court-involved youth because of the ability to place youth in remedial classes. This is particularly important when youth have received education in residential facilities that may not be up to par with state education standards of public schools.

Finally, youth with a disability, such as a significant mental health diagnosis but does not rise to the level of need under special education, are eligible for the consideration of creating a 504 Plan. This 504 Plan is typically a one-to-two-page document stating the diagnosis, observations in the classroom, strengths, weaknesses, and low level general education classroom accommodations to help the youth be successful and maintain positively in the classroom.

As it relates to discipline, youth under the special education program have additional mandatory steps before an expulsion is pursued. A special education youth referred for expulsion is afforded a Manifestation Determination meeting conducted by home school in coordination with the district special education department to determine if the behavior was or was not a result of the disability. If school staff determines the behavior was a result of the disability, the team revises the IEP, conducts a Function Behavior Assessment (FBA), and creates/modifies a behavior plan for the youth based on the results of the FBA. If the behavior was not a manifestation of the disability, school now has the option to proceed with an expulsion if they choose.

The most important piece to remember is that school district special education staff must be notified and involved on every special education case in the ES caseload.

For more information in Colorado about RtI, special education law, and related services visit the following websites:

Colorado Department of Education: www.cde.state.co.us
Rocky Mountain Children's Law Center: www.childlawcenter.org
The Arc of Adams County: www.arcadams.org

ESL/ESS (English Second Language or English Language Learners)

When a youth is fluent in more than one language, it is important to consider the need for ESL services. Youth are tested for ESL services when their home language survey enrollment document indicates that another language other than English is spoken at home and/or youth learned another language first prior to learning English. More concerning is the low achievement rates of Hispanic youth who have not obtained English language proficiency by ninth grade found in a study out of the University of Chicago (Gwynne et al., 2012). It was found in this same study that Hispanic youth, "may be much less well prepared for educational opportunities beyond high school than white and Asian students" (p. 4).

As a result, specific attention should be given to high school youth who are not proficient in English if they have received services since elementary school or newly identified ESL adolescent age youth. Please be aware that sometimes special education needs can be masked by the English language barrier. Be sure to ask the youth about previous ESL services and inform the new school of any ESL specific concerns. The youth may know his/her ESL proficiency levels and it is important to notify the new school to conduct testing at time of enrollment if necessary. Testing is conducted each year to assess ESL proficiency. Testing records should be valid for one school year and follow the youth with every school move. For outside agencies, it is important to note that the youth my not understand English well but not reveal as much. This results in a possible lack of compliance due to not fully understanding legal proceedings and expectations.

Behavior/Discipline History Including Expulsions

When requesting records, the ES must request behavior records and check for any current expulsions from the school district if the youth is not enrolled. This is particularly important for juvenile justice youth when an offense may have occurred on school grounds. If a youth is expelled from a school district, all districts in the state can choose to uphold that expulsion and refuse entrance until the expulsion term ends. The expelling district is responsible for providing any type of expulsion services such as an online program either in the home or at a centralized location. If the youth moves into a new district during the expulsion period and transportation to the expulsion program is difficult, the new school district may be willing to provide courtesy expulsion services at their program but are certainly not required to do so.

For special education students, when a student is expelled, the expulsion program modifies the IEP to reflect new placement and service hours during the expulsion term such as homebound services with a homebound instructor. Be sure to request the most recent IEP since expulsion. One might find the IEP is not current if the youth has not been enrolled in school for a significant period of time and this needs to be disclosed upon application to new schools. The IEP must be updated upon entrance into the new school. Depending on the expulsion, the youth may have certain alternative school options available even while under an active expulsion. Charter and independent alternative schools have the choice to accept a youth under expulsion and some that specialize in working with at-risk youth will take that chance to interview and accept a youth under expulsion. Many, however, will hesitate to enroll if the expulsion is a weapons charge on or off school grounds. Outside agencies must plan carefully and be honest with schools when seeking enrollment for a youth with this type of offense. School safety is of the utmost importance for all youth. It can ultimately depend on the type and details of the weapons offense and each case should be treated individually.-

Sexual Offenses

Any youth who is adjudicated on a sexual offense will be required to comply with an Individualized Supervision and Management Plan (ISMP) within the school building. This plan is facilitated by the probation officer, informed supervisor school district staff, building staff, caseworker, and any active therapist involved in the case. Refer to the State Sex Offender Management Board for specific guidance on school guidelines and rules.

Truancy

Youth may have experienced difficulty attending school in the past for many different reasons. These reasons range from dependency, neglect, abuse, mobility, juvenile delinquency, lack of motivation, and many others. When the ES requests records and inquiring to expulsion status, the ES should inquire truancy status as well. The school district may have an active truancy case and an assigned truancy liaison. It is helpful to speak with this truancy liaison about family background, dynamic, and service history through the district. This creates another venue for sharing information on new cases that might provide insightful information on family for both agencies and schools moving forward.

Homeless Youth (McKinney-Vento Act)

In Colorado, a youth maintains the right to attend school where he/she lives with parent/guardian (home school district) with a proof of residency. However, some families in our systems are homeless. Under McKinney-Vento Act, these youth are protected as they are considered "homeless" and can continue to attend their home school with or without proof of residency. When a youth currently lacks a permanent home, lives in a temporary shelter, car, abandoned building, is "kicked out of home," considered a run away, or is living with friends/relatives due to a lack of stable residency, this youth is technically homeless. In Colorado, it was determined that youth who are awaiting foster care placement do not fall under McKinney Vento because Colorado no longer utilizes temporary receiving homes. This may vary state to state so be sure to clarify local laws within the action team.

Under this law, the youth maintains the right to attend the same school he/she attended prior to becoming homeless (school of origin) even if youth has since moved to a new home. Thus, youth can stay in the school of origin for the remainder of the school year if the youth chooses to do so. For additional support, each school district employs a "McKinney-Vento Homeless Liaison" who can offer resources financially and administratively. If any youth experiences homelessness, it behooves the ES to contact the homeless liaison directly to assist in providing educational services and support. In Colorado, the Colorado Department of Education maintains a list of homeless liaisons at www.cde.state.co.us/dropoutprevention/homeless_liaisons. Action teams in other states are encouraged to visit state education websites for more information and contacts.

Chapter 20

Incorporating Into Current Practices

Direct educational planning is traditionally not considered a first priority when placing a youth out of the home whether due to dependency and neglect or a "beyond control of parent" situation. However, a few simple steps in the forefront of a case can make the difference in a youth's educational success long-term. The following outlines steps in individualized educational planning when a youth becomes involved with child welfare with the creation of an ES position. This outline serves as a sample to be individualized for the position and county in which it is implemented. To review up until this point, in the action team, child welfare has identified the exact process and steps that take place when a youth becomes involved with the system and/or is removed from home. With this knowledge and working in coordination with child welfare supervisors, the action team has identified where these steps will fit into the process in every single case. Child welfare departments in partnership with action teams have identified which staff will initiate BID meetings, educational notification to schools, and notifications or referrals to the ES for direct service. Without an ES, the county may only implement certain direct services pieces that are realistic for the staff to implement in addition to current duties. Note that those who implement ES positions see greater success and more academic consistency for youth. For example, an ES can initiate BID meetings on every single case and given that this is a new requirement of Every Student Succeeds Act (ESSA), it behooves a county to have a dedicated position implement standard practices. This helps ensure BID meetings are initiated consistently and with objectivity among caseworkers. This is simply one example of improved processes by way of the creation of an ES position. There are examples of education direct service procedures in states such as Washington, Illinois, and California for both child welfare and juvenile justice. These locations have established an education specific unit within the system level to provide direct service. It is strongly encouraged that the action team review these manuals and systems to compare with the current level of service in the county and possibly state.

Training New Education Direct Service Staff

When a new ES position is implemented, the action team should take time to write out a training procedure for the ES to become accustomed to the agencies, courts, and schools in which he/she will be interfacing. A training outline should be developed by the action team including ways in which the ES can initiate meeting with child welfare, probation departments, diversion departments, pre-trial agencies, juvenile assessment centers, local mental health, courts, and local school districts to learn systems in which he/she will be implementing education direct service as a new position. Consider all school and agency training in which the ES may benefit. This may mean the ES attends new caseworker training for child welfare, CASA training, new probation officer training, and so on. Arrange for the ES to meet with the main action team members who are most involved in educational planning for court-involved youth. The ES should take time to research alternative and charter options in the county and to meet with the administration of these schools to build relationships. The ES should learn more about what qualifies a youth to attend certain schools, enrollment windows, eligibility criteria, typical student portrait, discipline policies, credit recovery options, and overall school culture of most utilized schools. By the time the ES is fully implemented, he/she has a clear understanding of all school options, general and special education law, and the inner working of agencies interfacing with youth on a daily basis and is able to explain these systems to families in how it will impact academics. Often, the ES will need to explain agency policies to school staff and school policies to agency staff. It is an integral part of being the point of contact providing education direct service to court-involved youth as the systems have not typically interacted consistently.

Chapter 21

Roles and Responsibilities of Agencies and Schools

Each agency has a unique role in the educational planning for youth. To fully understand the flow of educational direct service, the agency/school responsibilities must be reviewed. This is a comprehensive list that also applies to juvenile justice youth as well and will not be repeated. Listed below are potential roles and responsibilities for each agency direct service staff. This listing of responsibilities is in addition to the responsibilities for transition planning. Roles for both juvenile justice and child welfare involvement are similar and are not separated.

School Responsibility:

- Provide all records to ES including attendance, birth certificate, immunizations, behavior, testing scores, ESL proficiency, transcripts, special education records, 504 plans, and/or behavior plans.
- Participation in school ISMP creation with supervising agency if youth has a sexual offense.
- Enroll foster care youth with or without records and obtain records within ten days from ES or CWEL from home school district.
- Ensure IEP is up to date.
- Respond timely to SPED requests and requests for meetings on any youth.
- Communication of academic or behavior concerns to youth team.
- School safety for client and ALL youth in school.
- Keep youth connected to home school positive peers and adults.

Other important school staff:

Special Education Out of District Coordinators: This position is responsible for SPED youth transition in and out of district schools from residential facilities. Coordinators also are responsible for requesting educational funding for youth in day treatment or residential.

Student Services Director/Intervention Services: This position can be utilized when a public school is not being cooperative with timely enrollment or "refusing" youth. The position often oversees discipline/expulsion and gives approval to schools seeking to move forward with expulsion on individual youth. It behooves an ES to connect and develop an effective working relationship with this person to more collaboratively plan for expelled youth.

Special Education Coordinator: This position assists in connecting the ES to individual SPED staff in community schools that are working directly with youth. This position is also helpful when school staff are not responsive and/or immediate intervention is necessary.

Teachers: The Juvenile Law Center and Education Law Center (2012) indicates six things a teacher can do to help a youth succeed in a new school. These include:

- Welcome youth to the school (tour of school, check in with youth regularly, ensure all school supplies) while being mindful not to disclose child welfare involvement for those who do not need to know.
- Ensure adult support for the youth's education (counselor, mentor, positive activities).
- Engage the youth in school community and activities (conversation with youth about interests and support in getting involved).
- Be an advocate for the most appropriate education (if youth needs additional support, larger or smaller settings and/or special education, remedial classes, behavior plan, 504, etc.).
- Address the behavioral and physical health needs of the youth (consider trauma in this evaluation of services).
- Help older youth plan for post-secondary education (assistance with process of applying and financial aid).

Agency Responsibility:

For foster youth: Child welfare caseworker
For juvenile justice youth: Pre-trial, probation, or parole officer
For crossover youth: Child welfare case worker

- Keep all enrollment documents in a central location.
- Assist with transportation to home school when removed from home.
- Lead facilitation of ISMP meeting for youth with sexual offenses.
- Notify ES and participate in BID meetings to discuss a youth staying in the current school each time a change in living environments occurs.
- Include school staff in planning and collaboration of services.
- Provide pertinent information on youth that may impact academic performance with discretion.
- Get to know a youth's individual motivation and goals and speak up to other team members if there are concerns.
- Facilitate communication how mental health and trauma may impact learning in individual cases.
- Give school contact/CWEL advanced notice of pending school changes.
- Participate and eventually take the lead on school progress meetings for team to discuss options and progress once an ES closes the case.

Guardian Ad Litem (GAL) Responsibility:

- Knowledgeable about the educational needs of the individual youth to best advocate objectively.
- Advocate for appropriate education services in community schools.
- Participate in BID meetings to discuss a youth staying in home school each time a change in living environments occurs.
- Act as an Educational Surrogate Parent if the youth needs an adult to maintain educational signing rights.
- Utilized legal background and knowledge of education law to advocate for youth.
- Provide adult mentorship in engaging youth in academics to pursue a diploma or GED.

Court Responsibility:

- Provide oversight of all teams working with youth on educational attainment.
- Assist in creating a culture of educational importance at each court hearing.
- Ask education-related questions at every follow-up court date for child welfare, crossover, and juvenile justice cases.

Parent/Guardian and/or Foster Parent Responsibility:

- Sign release of information at point of intake for both general and special education records and maintain education file.
- Promote education at home.
- Attend all school meetings.
- Engage in active collaboration and communication with new or current school.
- If necessary, take the lead on submitting a written request for a formal special education evaluation.
- Visit potential new schools with adolescent age youth looking to re-engage in school.

Youth Responsibility:

- Daily attendance.
- Older youth have a responsibility to show commitment and motivation.
- Commitment to personal goals.
- Communicate their academic needs to the youth team.
- Ask for help.
- Create short-term academic goals and review regularly.
- Advocate for self to participate in pro-social groups and/or sports at school.

Chapter 22

Procedures for Educational Direct Service for Child Welfare and Juvenile Justice

Below describes each step of the ES direct service process. The type of case will determine the next steps in educational planning. There are two separate tracks with the possibility that a client will be involved in both systems (crossover youth). In this case, depending on the agency that notified ES of involvement will determine initial educational planning steps. If the notification came from child welfare, utilize the child welfare educational planning procedures and adapt to fit the county specific needs. If referral/notification came from juvenile justice, utilize educational planning procedures specific to juvenile justice youth. There is a sample outline of both procedures in this section. It is now the responsibility of the ES and the action team to adapt the procedures below to fit the county specific process, needs, and resources, thus drafting personalized ES procedures.

Child Welfare Track

STEP ONE: ES Receipt of Notification of Child Welfare Involvement
This process is now established from the systems to trigger ES involvement and educational planning.

STEP TWO: Gather records
Once a notification or referral is received, all related school enrollment and special education documents are collected. A file is now created and the requirements are listed for the youth file once a referral is made. Youth files are required to maintain educational information, records, and notes on the youth plan and progress as information is used for database entry. Examples of many of these forms are in the appendices. Be sure to request records from all placements, this is particularly important for high school age youth.

Required documents for file:

- Case file checklist
- Notification and/or referral form
- BID documents (may be multiple)
- Any academic progress reports
- All collected school related enrollment documents: Transcript, attendance, discipline history, immunizations, and birth certificate

- All special education documents: eligibility (if available and most recent IEP) kept electronically
- Case progress notes and a service log to document service time
- Educational Intake form
- Parent Interview

Other related documents for file:

- Transition and/or discharge summary
- GED checklist
- Education Success Plan completed and updated versions
- Weekly attendance from school and any additional behavioral documents that arise
- Education passport
- Goal tracking worksheets

STEP THREE: Best Interest Determination Participation
The ES will either facilitate or actively participate in BID meetings depending on how the action team writes this position into the BID procedures described in phase 2. Per the family code, the state mandates this meeting happen within a particular timeframe and the ES should ensure this occurs consistently each time in collaboration with the CWEL. The ES takes responsibility for BID meetings once open on the case to ensure these meetings happen with every change of home placement.

STEP FOUR: Database Entry and Reporting
The ES should create a simple database to track client caseload and positive/negative/neutral discharges. This will allow the ES to easily track outcomes data to show effectiveness of services. The ES will follow up in checking attendance for closed cases one, three, and six months following closure. It is worth keeping this specific database at first to easily track client data for the first year in how the ES is utilized, where time is spent most effectively, and any difference in outcomes for those receiving educational services from the ES compared with those not receiving services. An example of the ES database should include but is not limited to:

Case number assignment
Date of referral
Last/first name
Date of birth
School of origin
Home school district
Child welfare caseworker (keep this up to date as it may change)
ES closure date
Checkbox for special education
Checkbox for crossover youth
Checkbox for ESL

BID meeting date and decision
Sessions total (time spent on case such as school meetings, interviews, individual time with youth, BID meetings)
School status (expelled, truant, dropout, or good standing)
Special notes

In the first year, the Douglas County Educational Navigator tracked specific education services such as the total number of school meetings, expulsion hearings, and BID meetings occurring for each student so as to identify where time was most spent. This tracking also allowed the ES to report on how many youth remained or were removed from home school.

STEP FIVE: Educational Intake Form
An educational intake form sample document is included in this guide. This form was created in PDF and can be done in print or digital format. This intake form is utilized by the ES when a youth file is created, and a youth is now on an ES caseload for the purposes of educational planning or monitoring. It is important to always do this intake regardless of the youth status in current school. As a first step, the intake acts as baseline for academic sustainability and growth. With this initial information, supports to prevent any academic decline can be put in place in the start of a case. With a baseline of academic information, it is now easier to see if youth exhibits any type of academic decline and intervene immediately. Oftentimes, if the educational intake is not done initially, academic/behavioral problems can arise that were not identified immediately because staff did not conduct an intake of education needs. It is a disservice to youth if professionals do not fully evaluate academic needs immediately upon entrance into the child welfare system.

For child welfare youth, the ES will see a range of academic progress. In some cases, a youth may be doing very well in school and the intake acts as a baseline to track educational stability. This intake is also helpful for facilities or foster parents who are learning about their new youth in efforts to maintain and encourage academic growth. In other situations, the need for planning and intervention will be evident immediately. The intake then ensures that education is a top priority in treatment planning for youth and family. It is the one service that is not done consistently for court-involved youth. All too often, education issues are not considered as of equal importance in a youth case. This paradigm shift must happen to ensure youth teams are meeting the educational needs for all court-involved youth.

STEP SIX: Academic Monitoring and Supplemental Funding

Child Welfare Community School Academic Monitoring

If youth move schools after out of home removal as a result of a BID decision, be conscious of the timing of the school move. Consider the importance particularly for adolescent youth in finishing a school term in current school before transitioning into new school. ES can organize a new school enrollment meeting if the youth team deems it necessary. Some youth may not want this, they may not want the attention, and the ES can see to it that, regardless of the youth's preference, the youth feels supported and knows the ES is advocating for their best interest. Youth staying in home school may or may not need a school progress meeting at home school. It is up to the youth team to determine next steps taking into account the trauma that might have ensued with a removal from the home. If a meeting is requested by any team member, the ES can organize and facilitate this meeting. At this time, an Education Success Plan can be written with the team and youth. If the youth identifies goals on which to work, these are noted on the success plan and updated at each meeting thereafter. A sample Education Success Plan and goals worksheet are located in the appendices. Consider these documents a baseline on which to expand and personalize. With a new school placement, the ES should ensure that the youth gets to know new school staff and starts to build positive connections. The ES can share the most relevant information to establish the youth in a new school successfully. The ES can ensure that the IEP or 504 plan is implemented and that youth knows the intention and accommodations listed in these documents. After the intake is done, the ES will monitor progress weekly connecting with the youth team including school staff with updates on attendance, grades, and behaviors.

Child Welfare Facility Academic Monitoring

First and foremost, always consider maintaining youth in home school while in a facility and conduct a BID as soon as possible. In the meantime, if youth is enrolled, youth should attend home school until the BID occurs. The CWEL can notify home school of facility home placement. However, if youth goes into a facility school, the ES can send all educational records to the facility and request to be a part of the initial facility staffing. The ES will conduct an educational intake of youth within the first month of facility placement so as to ensure academic needs are addressed during that first staffing. It is then the responsibility of the youth team to create educational goals with the help of the ES along with treatment goals during the initial meeting. If youth is in facility but the best interest is to stay in home school, the facility can partner with agencies and utilize funds to provide transportation to home school from the facility. Be sure to include the facility in the BID meeting to provide input on the decision and learn more about the academic needs of the youth. At this point, ES monitors academic progress weekly connecting with the youth team including school staff with updates on attendance, grades, and behavior. If at any point, child welfare decides to remove the youth from community school and place in facility, the ES already has a comprehensive view of academic needs as they transition in and out of facilities and participates accordingly to ensure academic progress continues as much as possible.

Supplemental Funding

Consider the financial supports available to foster youth to ensure continued academic progress. Fees for sports and academics are waived for foster care youth and should be considered to keep youth attached to the community school. Consideration should also be given to mentoring and tutoring if the youth displays academic deficit upon systems entry and/or experiences multiple school moves. Many schools and programs are collaborating to offer both mentoring and tutoring at the school level. Consider all options in community school to keep youth engaged and ensure the ES is aware of these resources.

STEP SEVEN: Parent/Guardian Engagement

Parent/guardian engagement is crucial in the process of re-engaging youth in school and/or keeping youth in one school long-term. Foster parent engagement and training is also covered in this section as well.

School to parent partnership is extremely important in a youth's academic success. It is always the hope that the parent will actively collaborate with school staff and is empowered to do so throughout the case in preparation for a successful closure. According to research provided by The PACER Center, Inc. (2000), parents feel most supported when agencies:

Treat them with respect and dignity validating that *you are the expert on your youth*;

Acknowledge that all families have strengths;

Are culturally sensitive, respect spiritual practices, and provide services accordingly;

Do not place blame on one single entity;

Professionals listen and do not judge;

Hold youth accountable for their behaviors;

Provide parent training;

Provide information rights, education, child welfare, and juvenile systems; and

Empower the parent to communicate with the school and advocate for the youth's academic and emotional needs.

(p. 1)

The parent, with the guidance of the ES, can learn how to effectively communicate and navigate the school system. This is, however, if the intention of the caseworker is for the foster youth to eventually return home to the parent/guardian. First, check with the caseworker to inquire the status of the parent and intention of services. If the goal is to return home, be sure to include the parent/guardian in any type of school meeting. This is particularly important if the youth is in special education. A biological parent that maintains educational signing rights must be present for all meetings and sign off on any special education decisions and testing. School staff will always do whatever they can to include the biological parent in all processes and all agencies should support parental attendance in whatever means necessary. If the biological parent cannot be located, it behooves professionals to appoint an Educational Surrogate Parent (ESP) to maintain signing rights for youth for all educational matters. This person should be someone with the best interest of the child in mind but cannot be a caseworker. Often, the GAL is appointed.

Foster Parent Engagement

It is important for foster parents to know the crucial transportation guidelines when a youth is placed in their care and know they may be called upon to provide that transportation in the interim while long-term transportation is put in place. Foster parents also have a responsibility to encourage a youth in education and set an overall encouraging home environment to promote educational success. It is the responsibility of the county and ES to organize foster parent training on education rights, expectations of youth in their care, general and special education law, education advocacy, special needs of youth in care, and transition planning. Foster parents receive much training around certain topics concerning trauma and social/emotional health and should be equally trained in foster care youth education so they can effectively promote successful educational outcomes. Provided in the appendices is a "Help Foster Educational Success" handout, which can be given to a biological parent/guardian or a foster parent as it applies to both. To foster educational success parents are encouraged to:

- Set high expectations;
- Provide a supportive home environment;
- Monitor and provide help with homework;
- Praise school success and talents;
- Encourage a youth to participate in extracurricular activities and sports;
- Address special school-related costs;
- Attend parent/teacher conferences and stay connected to the school community;
- Support educational aspirations;
- Engage youth in conversations about future goals;
- Communicate with the caseworker.

If the youth is in special education, encourage parents to receive direct training about special education law and parental rights to better understand the entire special education system. Youth are afforded many rights not available to general education youth when they are involved in special education. As mentioned in phase 2, many parents are unfamiliar with this process and need specific training in this area. School district staff can often speak in IEP meetings assuming that parents and youth understand the special education language. During meetings, school staff should check for understanding and stop meetings to explain details if family members do not seem to understand. Best practice for professionals is to encourage parents/guardians to educate themselves about the youth's disabilities, help them develop a consistently structured parenting style appropriate to the disability, and provide information that explains due process rights and gives tips for advocating for youth in appropriate ways.

STEP EIGHT: Case Closure Procedures

Case closure is determined by the youth team and the ES. In the adapted procedures, the ES should indicate length of time a case stays open depending on the total number of youth on an ES caseload and the specific responsibilities of the position. Consideration to close in child welfare cases also depends on the stability of home placement. If home life and education placement are stable, the case can be considered for closure. In the 17th Judicial District, the Education Advocate keeps a case open for at least the first 45 days after the first school enrollment meeting, including at least one school progress meeting displaying positive progress and stability. The Educational Navigator in Douglas County maintains a different timeline for the closing of a case. The following are criteria for successful, unsuccessful, and neutral closure. Note successful and unsuccessful closures are not dependent on parent involvement as the youth may not return to the original home. Regardless, at the time of closure, youth shall be enrolled and attending school placement.

Successful Closure:

Youth is enrolled and attending.
Youth has not acquired criminal charges.
Youth has shown improved grades and behavior in school environment.
Youth has successfully engaged in credit recovery and/or tutoring.
Youth returns to family successfully.
Youth remains in home school successfully despite home removal.
Youth on track academically for age and grade.

Unsuccessful Closure:

Youth continues as a non-attender in school of enrollment.
Youth acquires criminal charges and/or truancy involvement.
Youth has not engaged and/or cooperated with the Education Plan.

Neutral Closure:

Youth denies need for educational assistance and/or uninterested.
Youth is a change of venue to another county.

STEP NINE: Data Collection

As mentioned above, at the time of closure, the youth shall be enrolled and attending school placement. At each time of follow-up data collection, it shall be verified that the youth is still enrolled and attending school. Follow-up data shall be collected at one, three, and six months (if possible) after case closure. ES may find it hard to track data at 6 months, but it shows sustained school stability, and more importantly, validates the educational direct service position. Tracking outcomes for negative discharges may show trends in negative outcomes based on a lack of engagement in school such as juvenile justice involvement later in life. Agencies must agree on a consistent way in which to track these youth long term. Keep in mind, this step depends on the action team decision as to how long an ES should track cases. The action team can decide to keep ES open on cases until the child welfare case closes, which is feasible with smaller caseloads or counties where the number of child welfare youth is manageable for one ES position to provide the direct service described here. The action team should write into procedures, the size of an ES caseload, and specify the level of direct service provided given recommendations of phase 3.

In any case, should additional needs arise for educational services, the ES in collaboration with the youth team determines if a case is re-opened. In this situation, the ES shall note new case open/close dates and treat as a new case and track outcomes accordingly. The ES shall obtain a new release from the family to ensure open communication and there is a new release signed at the time of referral.

Juvenile Justice Track

STEP ONE: Initial Notification/Referral of Juvenile Justice Involvement
Not all juvenile justice youth will need direct educational planning; however, preventative measures are very important as youth may appear to be doing quite well in school when charges are accrued. Other juvenile justice youth will need a tremendous amount of planning, support, and re-engagement immediately at the start of a case. To this end, the way to involve school district staff in individual educational planning will vary county to county. The action team should consider having both an automatic notification of involvement and also a referral process if the ES does not get involved for whatever reason upon notification, any juvenile justice staff can make a referral later in the case. A referral can be generated by way of many different avenues: the juvenile assessment center when conducting initial intake, pre-trial supervision officers, probation officers, judge/magistrate court order involvement, child welfare case workers, GALs, and public defenders. All staff capable of making a referral should be made aware of this process and be provided appropriate documents to make a referral, including the release form necessary from the family. The referral form should include a release form that must be signed by a parent at time of notification of referral for services. This notifies the parent that the ES will contact the family and that the parent gives full access to the ES of all educational records from all school placements. This release prevents any potential barriers in communication with all parties and is always best practice.

STEP TWO: Gather Educational Records
Once a notification or referral is received, all related school enrollment and special education documents are collected. A file is now created and the requirements are listed for the youth file once a referral is made. Youth files are required

to maintain educational information, records, and notes on the youth plan and progress as information is used for database entry. Examples of certain forms are in the appendices.

Required documents for file:

- Case file checklist
- Notification and/or referral form
- BID documents (may be multiple)
- ES court reports
- HIPAA compliant release form signed by parent
- All collected school related enrollment documents: Transcript, attendance, discipline history, immunizations, and birth certificate
- All special education documents: Eligibility (if available and most recent IEP) or 504 plan kept electronically
- Case progress notes and a service log to document time spent on case
- Educational Intake form
- Parent Interview

Other Related Documents for file (but not limited to):

- Transition summary
- GED checklist towards all necessary steps to take final exam
- Education Success Plan completed and updated versions from additional progress meetings
- Weekly attendance from school and any additional behavior reports that arise
- Education passport
- Expulsion letters
- Behavior plans
- FBA (Functional Behavior Assessment)
- Threat assessments

STEP THREE: Database Entry and Reporting

The ES should create a simple database to track client caseload and positive/negative/neutral discharges. This will allow the ES to easily track outcomes data to show effectiveness of services. It is worth keeping this database separate initially to separately track client data for the first year in how the ES is utilized, where time is spent most effectively and any difference in outcomes for those receiving educational services from the ES compared with those not receiving services. This is particularly important in juvenile justice where action teams can monitor recidivism rates for those youth accepting or declining education services. An example of the ES database should include but is not limited to:

Case number assignment
Date of referral
Last/first name

DOB
School of origin
Home school district
Referring person (may be county attorney, PD, court, ACHSD, or PO/pre-trial
    or school)
Child welfare worker
ES closure date
Sessions total (time spent on case noted in a file service log)
School status (expelled, truant, dropout, or engaged)
Special notes

STEP FOUR: Educational Intake

An educational intake form sample document is included in this guide. This form was created in PDF and can be completed in print or digital format. This intake form is utilized by the ES when a youth file is created, and a youth is now on an ES caseload for the purposes of educational planning or monitoring. It is important to **always** do this intake regardless of the youth status in the current school. As a first step, the intake acts as baseline for academic sustainability and growth. With this initial information, supports are put in place to keep youth engaged. If the ES has a baseline of academic information, it is now easier to see if the youth exhibits any type of academic decline and intervene immediately.

For juvenile justice youth, there may be a significant academic history of disruption possibly stemming back to elementary school. An ES may find a youth has had significantly struggled academically and the offense may have occurred on school grounds. In this stage, the intake acts as a summary of academic barriers, strengths, and weaknesses to learn more about youth needs and motivation to begin the process of school opportunities and re-engagement. Finally, the intake will help identify appropriate educational goals in conjunction with the youth.

Specifically for juvenile justice, part of the intake is to conduct a parent interview. A sample of which is provided in the appendices. Also, it is helpful for the ES to contact former or current school staff working with youth. Often, the youth/family version of school events differs from events noted by school staff. Establishing a partnership with school staff and understanding their experience with the family/youth is part of the ES position. As an added benefit, this process of connecting with former or current school staff will allow the identification of the type of relationship between family/school that is either helping or hindering positive educational outcomes.

Level of Services Decision

When records are obtained and interviews conducted, the ES decides the level of services necessary to ensure educational success. This may be direct educational planning and meetings frequently with youth to monitor progress either closely in person with youth and/or electronically via email each week. If a youth is not engaged in the process and does not want direct service support, a simple list of resources and school options can be included in a folder with all enrollment documents for the youth to seek enrollment in a school of their choice. In many cases, referrals are sent for youth whom agencies hope to re-engage in school and believe assistance by the ES will promote enrollment. Youth often do not know what options are available to them and have lost all hope until speaking to an individual who is well aware of the potential schools that will meet their individual needs. This conversation alone often sparks a youth's interest in re-engagement in his/her education goals.

However, in speaking to youth and family, if the youth is not vested in this endeavor and conversations with the ES does not spark an interest by the youth then it does not behoove the youth or the ES to continue involvement. The ES will make this determination while conducting initial intakes and explain to the referral party why a case will not open. While it is always a requirement of probation that a youth be either in school or obtain employment full time, the ES cannot force the youth to take advantage of educational services. In any event, youth walk away with a new awareness of schooling options should they choose to engage at a later time. The ES should not be put in a punitive position so as to recommend consequences for the youth for failure to participate in educational services. The ES is a mediator between agencies/schools and families to ensure all parties are communicating and working effectively. It is not the job of the ES to issue consequences for youth but rather notify the supervising agencies of progress or lack thereof. The ES is to stay neutral throughout the case to keep trusting relationships with agencies, families, youth, and schools.

STEP FIVE: Home School Progress Meeting or School Progress Monitoring
This next step will depend on the needs, strengths, academic standing, and the information taken from the educational intake. Youth staying in home school may or may not need a school progress meeting at home school. It is up to the youth team to determine the next steps. The ES may be involved after intake to simply monitor progress and attendance if the youth is in good standing. If a meeting is requested by any team member, the ES can organize and facilitate this meeting. At this time, an Education Success Plan can be written with the team and youth. If the youth identifies short-term goals on which to work, these are noted on the success plan and updated at each meeting thereafter. The action team will need to decide if the ES or the supervising agency monitors the short-term goals youth identifies at a school progress meeting. Provided in the appendices is a Goal Tracking Sheet for the ES/supervising agency to track throughout the school year with additional space to create new goals. This level of involvement of the ES truly depends on the ES caseload. If the ES has the time built in to the position to meet with youth regularly at school, then it is best that the ES tracks these goals with youth. If the ES position has a larger caseload such as the 17th Judicial District Education Advocate, then encourage the supervising agency to take over school progress meetings and track education goals along with treatment goals at monthly meetings with youth.

STEP SIX: Schooling Options (Matching the Right Student with the Right School) Once the intake is conducted and records collected, utilize family demographics and the youth's academic eligibility to explore school options. Certain academic statuses of youth may determine what schools are viable options. The hope is that youth can interview with particular schools that will meet the identified academic needs, help youth feel supported, offer credit recovery, and welcome the youth into the community. Within the county, there are a variety of schooling options available to youth including home school, alternative district schools, charter schools, home schooling, and online schooling. The combination of school eligibility, SPED status, transportation, credit achieved, time of year, and youth engagement will determine which school will fit the youth. As the ES grows into the position and develops working relationships with school staff, he/she will know about all available options in the area that have specific application processes, unique school cultures, and work well with certain youth. In addition, the youth's status within a district will dictate what options are available. Below is a list of possible youth statuses that can impact educational options.

Special Consideration: School Eligibility Status
Expulsion Status

If a youth is expelled for a minor offense, it is possible that specific charter schools particularly hybrid classroom environments will be willing to consider the youth application pending an interview. A hybrid learning environment can range from online learning at home, learning labs, and/or in combination with classroom instruction. If the expulsion is a serious offense such as a weapons charge, one can expect that youth will only be eligible for expulsion services through the expelling district. An enrollment meeting can be set with the expulsion program to set-up services and establish expectations and communication in monitoring progress through the remainder of the expulsion. While professionals hope that home school will find creative ways to work with juvenile justice youth, there is no absolute right to attend a neighborhood school within a school district and the district ultimately has discretion given current criminal status as to what options are available to youth. If the school district feels the youth poses a threat to the safety of other students and staff via a threat assessment, weapons charges, or current expulsion, the district has the option of referring the youth to alternative options. A school district has the right to base a denial of admission or referral to an alternative setting on criminal behavior within the previous 12 months. Within phase 2, school staff train agencies on school procedures, including discipline, so the ES will know how the school districts in the county choose to implement education law.

Good Standing Status

If a youth is a dropout and/or otherwise needs re-engagement or support in the current or new school, the ES should work to explore options both in the home district and outside charter programs. Options should be matched based on address, credit status, grade level, application requirements, available academic support, transportation, and connection to the school community. If the youth is low on credits, it will behoove the youth to look for modified diploma programs and seek credit recovery programs in the area. It is important to determine what the youth is working toward (i.e., employment, college, trade) and how the youth plans to utilize the high school diploma. Engaging in these conversations and exploring options further promotes the youth taking ownership of academic goals. This will help the team explore different ways to offer incentives and foster motivation in youth. ES should be realistic about what school options fit the youth's needs and are within transportation limits of family/youth. Even with good academic standing, if the youth discipline history and grades show a continued struggle in academics either behaviorally and/or academically, it is important to cover the possibility of conducting a special education evaluation in the chosen school setting. If the youth has a mental health disability and there is a chance that this disability is interfering with classroom progress, a 504 eligibility meeting is also important to consider. Ensure to foster the four academic mindsets within the new school to sustain educational success once the youth is enrolled, particularly the one that is most in need of attention.

STEP SEVEN: School Enrollment and Academic Monitoring
Once the youth and team pick the schools that are potentially a good fit for youth needs, it is time to visit the schools. If only one option is available due to various reasons stated above, this meeting is then a direct school meeting set by the ES. Otherwise, if multiple options are available, the ES proceeds with setting school meetings in line with proper enrollment dates for when a youth can start in the school (based on school calendar). These meetings are a chance for youth/family to interview the school as well for the school to interview the youth. Depending on youth eligibility, the number of school meetings will vary as the youth may want to consider multiple schools. Once a school enrollment decision is made, the youth submits enrollment paperwork and a follow-up enrollment meeting is set. During this enrollment meeting, an Education Success Plan or the like is created with the school, family, youth, and the team, outlining terms of successful participation and supports. The plan also includes **youth identified** short-term goals.

Next, the team sets the first school progress meeting anywhere from 7 to 30 days following the start date. This first date is decided at the time of the school enrollment meeting and continuation of these meetings is decided thereafter. If youth, family, and team feels that the meetings are helpful, these meetings are encouraged to continue. Some teams may decide to meet monthly, quarterly, or at semester end. Whatever the decision, it is most importantly individualized to fit what the youth finds helpful. Finally, the ES collects all email addresses from all parties involved so that school, agencies, and the parent/guardian can stay in regular contact about the youth. The ES sends the Education Success Plan or the like electronically to all parties via email following the initial meeting, thus initiating long-term communication of all parties.

If the ES has a smaller caseload, consider this position availability to meet with the youth regularly at the school campus anywhere from every one to three weeks to build a working relationship with the youth and continued encouragement to attend school regularly. Invite school staff to participate in these ES meetings with youth so as to build that positive school connection as well. Some youth will like regular check-ins either by phone or in person while others will not find it helpful.

Special Consideration
Juvenile Justice and Court Decisions

In some situations, school will be interrupted for the youth and the ES must be aware of all scenarios where the youth's consistent school attendance and credit accumulation is impacted. Keep in mind that court-involved youth have outside factors influencing academic outcomes. Youth may be removed from school regardless of academic progress if:

- Youth receives new criminal charges;
- Youth is arrested and placed in detention;
- Youth is revoked on probation or pre-trial and placed in detention;
- Youth is removed from home and placed in residential care;
- Youth is placed in inpatient residential care for substance abuse; and
- Youth is sentenced to Division of Youth Corrections and placed in a residential facility.

In these scenarios, with the exception of a commitment sentence, the ES stays involved, keeps home school involved, advocates for the youth to stay in home school when possible, obtains transcripts from all placements, and maintains all educational transcripts amidst placement moves, planning accordingly when the youth is stable in community once again. If youth is committed to corrections, the ES can send records to new case manager and close services.

Length of ES Involvement

The county will need to decide if the ES or the supervising agency monitors the short-term goals the youth identifies at the school progress meeting and outline this procedure within the ES adapted count specific procedures. This will help determine length and intensity of ES services. Level of involvement of the ES truly depends on total ES caseload. If the ES has the time built in to the position to meet with the youth regularly at school, then it is best that the ES tracks these goals with the youth. If the ES position has a larger caseload such as the 17th Judicial District Education Advocate, then the ES encourages the supervising agency to take over school progress meetings and track education goals along with other goals at monthly meetings with the youth.

Regardless of level of services, for the first 30–45 days after first school progress/enrollment meeting, the ES checks attendance and behavior weekly and requests academic updates from the school staff. If this progress monitoring yields a lack of improvement in academics or a behavioral incident, the ES should consider scheduling a school progress meeting immediately to convene all parties quickly. The ES shall consult with all members of a youth's team via email to obtain feedback on intervention strategies.

Supplemental Funding

The ES may find that additional services are necessary to ensure academic success. This may be assistance with school fees, sports, tutoring, mentoring, or academic supplies. In the adapted ES procedures, the juvenile justice agencies should outline available funding for supplemental education costs and by what means these funds shall be requested. The 17th Judicial District Education Advocate utilizes funds from Senate Bill 94 and certain criteria must be met for a funding request to be approved. The Education Advocate must submit a funding request to the Senate Bill 94 Coordinator. Additionally, in Colorado, the 17th Judicial District Probation Department can utilize flexible funds for educational costs such as GED classes for probation clients. The juvenile justice agencies should outline the eligibility criteria for those funds so the officers will know the procedure in which to request funds. Criteria for Senate Bill 94 educational funds include one or more of the following:

- Youth has a probation officer or pre-trial case manager and is SB94 eligible;
- Youth shows a noticeable commitment to education either on a high school diploma or GED track;
- Youth needs assistance in a specific subject area to increase skills to grade level;
- Youth requires specific assistance to re-engage academically;
- Youth is in need of positive activities to stay connected to the school environment;
- Youth is showing improved attendance in school setting in which he/she is enrolled;
- Youth family does not have the additional monies to fully fund a school related fee and/or service; and
- Youth is showing consistent positive behavior in a traditional or alternative school setting.

STEP EIGHT: Parent/Guardian and/or Foster Parent Engagement

Just as within child welfare cases, parent/guardian engagement is extremely important in educational planning. Often, parents of juvenile delinquents need additional support in not only understanding the educational system but also the juvenile justice system as well. Professionals often see that families do not understand the discipline/expulsion policies, nor do they fully understand the difference between suspensions, being "kicked out," expulsions, or withdrawal for non-attendance. For whatever reason, communication between schools and parents often breaks down by the time the youth is involved in the juvenile justice system. It may be a language barrier, misunderstanding, disagreement with school staff, or perhaps the parent has just not engaged in a youth's education. Whatever the case, it is important for the ES to include the parent/guardian in all educational planning and school meetings. As mentioned in the step-by-step process, the ES contacts the parent and conducts a parent interview to gain insight into the academic history, needs, and strengths of the youth from the unique parent viewpoint. The 17th Judicial District Education Advocate often conducts the youth intakes and the parent intake separately so as to gain both individual perspectives without the other interfering. Often, parents/guardians wish to say things they do not want to say in front of their youth and vice versa. It is often helpful to then meet as a team with probation officer, family, and the youth to discuss further options once both intakes are completed. This limits any duplication of services and possibility of miscommunication.

When working with parents/guardians, encourage, validate, and empower parents to partner with agencies for the youth's success. Encourage them to be the major decision makers in the process of educational and/or transition planning. Gomperts (2014) suggests that youth are trying to make connections to adults whenever possible. As a result, however tumultuous a parent/guardian relationship to the youth might be in teenage years, professionals should encourage a youth to re-connect with a parent/guardian and provide supports in doing so. In addition to empowering parent/guardians in educational planning, select mentoring and tutoring programs that engage not only the youth but the family as well. This can have a positive impact on the family unit as they start to see the parent/guardian as a positive support. Encouragement for parent/guardian connection is evident in the literature as well, as Osher et al. (2012) also recommend that professionals connect youth to caring adults, mentors, and/or family members. Alvarado and Kumpfer (2000) suggest "parent supervision, attachment to parents, and consistency in discipline are the most important protective factors in promoting resilience to delinquency in high risk youth" (p. 1). Just as one might need to repair the relationship of the family to the school staff, one might, in the process, strengthen the relationship with parent/guardian to youth as all parties begin to take accountability for actions and contribute positively to the educational planning process.

As mentioned, the ES will have cases in which parent and school staff communication is broken down. That means the ES might need to repair that family communication with home school or foster collaboration in a new school in a positive way to prevent future misunderstandings. Parents and guardians often benefit from knowing effective communication skills when talking with school staff. The Education Advocate utilizes a parent handout outlining all the ways in which parents can stay engaged in a youth's education. It is important to remember when setting up parent/guardian communication with a new school to include the parent/guardian in team emails about youth progress, connect the parent/guardian with the school website, parent portal online access, and give them all educational records so they can maintain an educational folder for all enrollment documents. Included in the appendices is a document titled "Enrollment Checklist" that can be added to the education folder outlining all of the documents that must be contained in the folder when the parent/guardian seeks to enroll the youth.

The 17th Judicial District Education Advocate initially creates an enrollment folder for family, which includes informational handouts for both the parent and the youth, enrollment checklist, and all initial education records. The Advocate gives this folder to the youth and parent/guardian while outlining what they need to contribute to the educational folder for future enrollment purposes.

Disengaged Parent/Guardian

Unfortunately, there are parents/guardians who are disengaged from the process and do not wish to partner with the ES in this process. It is helpful to engage these caregivers in conversations, validate their concerns, and actively listening to any perceived negative experiences thus far in the school system. The ES does not however, condone such disconnected behavior but instead encourage them to re-engage in a positive way despite negative experiences. If the youth is under 18, the parent/guardian must sign enrollment paperwork anytime the youth seeks to enroll in public school. If the parent/guardian is difficult to engage, ensure the youth has another positive adult to assist in this process such as a mentor, tutor, family friend, other family member, or a positive school staff member. At minimum, ensure the parent/guardian does their obligatory part in submitting and signing enrollment paperwork while engaging the youth in nurturing school staff relationships and other supportive adult role models.

Disengaged Youth Procedure

Should youth not engage in agreements and services written into the Education Success Plan after intervention is attempted, not fulfill attendance requirements, and experience continued defiance, then the supervising officer is informed. The ES and youth team determine the next steps and level of ES involvement if any. In addition, the youth status may change such as new charges, revocations, and/or home issues. If this is the case and the youth leaves the current school, the ES collects academic records from the most recent school and follows the case until the youth stabilizes. This entails maintaining academic records from placements, detention, schools, and creation of an educational passport to possibly follow the youth through multiple settings.

STEP NINE: Case Closure Procedures
Case closure is determined by the youth team and the ES. In adapted procedures, the ES should indicate length of time a case initially stays open. When the case is closed successfully, the youth shall be enrolled and attending school placement. At each time of follow-up data collection, it shall be verified that the youth is still enrolled and attending school. The following are criteria for successful, unsuccessful, and neutral closure.

Successful Closure:

Youth is enrolled and attending.
Youth has not acquired new charges.
Youth has shown improved grades and behavior in school environment.
Youth has successfully engaged in credit recovery and/or tutoring.
Youth terminates probation successfully.

Unsuccessful Closure:

Youth continues as a non-attender in school of enrollment.
Youth acquires new charges and/or truancy involvement.
Youth has not engaged and/or cooperated with the Education Plan.
Youth terminates probation unsuccessfully.

Neutral Closure:

Youth denies need for educational assistance and/or uninterested.
Youth is sentenced to Juvenile Corrections.
Youth moves with family and case is a change of venue to another county.

STEP TEN: Data Collection
As mentioned above, at the time of successful closure, the youth shall be enrolled and attending school placement. At each time of follow-up data collection, it shall be verified that the youth is still enrolled and attending school. Follow-up data shall be collected at one, three, and six months (if possible) after case closure. ES may find it hard to track data at six months, but it shows sustained school stability and more importantly validates the educational direct service position. Tracking outcomes for negative discharges may show trends in negative outcomes based on a lack of engagement in school such as recidivism rates for those youth who did not engage in services. Agencies should agree on a consistent way in which to track these youth long-term. In some case closure situations, the ability to track data will not be possible such as a commitment to corrections.

In any case, should additional needs arise for educational services, the ES in collaboration with the youth team determines if a case is re-opened. In this situation, the ES shall open a new case on the youth and track outcomes accordingly. The ES shall obtain a new release from the family to ensure open communication.

Grievance Procedures

The action team and the ES shall adapt grievance protocol should an outside agency or family member dispute any educational services provided in both the child welfare and juvenile justice system. This shall incorporate within the grievance protocol details on contacting the direct supervisor for the ES in the agency with contact information.

Chapter 23

Action Team

Long-Term Sustainability

Regular Functions

Once an action team is in place and has met all identified goals, the next step is long-term sustainability. The facilitator of this team should be either the ES or an agreed upon action team member. This facilitator makes a long-term commitment to continually improve educational planning with court-involved youth as this is an area of continued growth and improvement. This facilitator is responsible for updating points of contact each year, cross-agency training, and organizing quarterly meetings.

Quarterly meetings can now be used to:

Problem solve target areas;
Ensure regular cross-agency training;
Fostering new business relationships with school staff;
Sharing new agency information and resources;
Grant applications and allocating funding toward improving educational outcomes as needed by each agency;
Staffing of unique case scenarios;
Adapt to evolving best practices and disseminate most recent research.

Furthermore, the facilitator is responsible for keeping policies and procedures updated for yearly training while introducing and informing new points of contact for agencies.

The action team can also be utilized as a sounding board for the individuals providing direct education services. This person can bring cases to the team that have extenuating circumstances, do not fit within the policies and procedures, or amplifies another gap in service for the team to problem solve. Within this review, the action team can identify needed practice improvements across systems, and agency-level reviews to evaluate adherence to, and the impact of, cross-system protocols and agreements. It is another opportunity to document significant improvements in procedures, identify how streamlining educational planning is effective, document possible changes in recidivism rates, and share positive youth experiences.

Meetings Frequency

Establish meeting frequency based on the best interest of maintaining the education agenda and agreement by all members. It is not recommended that meetings occur less than quarterly. By meeting quarterly, the team ensures that information is regularly disseminated, cases are staffed, and contacts are regularly updated without a large lapse in time between updates. Thus directly impacting the educational success of youth when a problem in protocols arise or a training/information session is necessary. Consider having the ES send out regular education update emails concerning any new information or need to the action team members.

Point of Contact Sustainability

Establish guidelines around staff turnover and reappointing an action team contact if a member leaves their respective agency. This is written into the initial contract with each representative every time an agency provides a new point of contact to participate on the action team. All of these individuals are updated on the contact list yearly and this list is sent to all action team members.

Sustained Crossover Training

By committing to the action team, the team also commits to continue regular cross-agency training. Phase 2 covered all the aspects of establishing and sustaining cross-agency training for agencies and schools. It is mentioned here as it is a long-term regular function of the action team members. It is important not to lapse services in this area as regular staff turnover in every agency necessitates a need to reintroduce staff and foster continual collaborations on educational planning. No one agency can facilitate all of the education planning. If one of the service providers or schools is not practicing the same educational planning procedures, it can disrupt the flow of information and/or cause a duplication of services.

Final Takeaway

All-encompassing systemic change seems daunting at first. It is the hope of this author that the hands-on materials and step-by-step sample procedures provided in this guide help to break down a seemingly overwhelming process into tasks that are within reach. While aiming for large-scale changes is encouraged, know that implementing any piece of this framework will improve educational outcomes.

Have the courage to dream big knowing that systemic change will improve educational outcomes and create workload efficiencies in the long run. Anything a team or agency implements from this framework will positively impact the lives of our youth, and it only takes one individual to set change in motion and make a difference.

Appendix 1

Notification Document of Juvenile Justice Involvement

DATE: _____

Dear Child Welfare Education Liaison,

This letter is to notify you that, (Student's Name and DOB): _____ has visited the Assessment Center on: _____ This letter serves as notice of new or additional juvenile justice involvement. Parent was informed that this notification is provided.

This youth was arrested for: _____ ☐ N/A (Voluntary case)

The youth currently attends _____ (current or most recent school)

☐ School District ____ ☐ Public Schools ☐ Public Schools ☐ District Unknown
☐ School District ____ ☐ Public Schools ☐ Public Schools ☐ Other: _____
☐ School District ____ ☐ Public Schools ☐ Public Schools

Placement as a result of the assessment/screen is _____, to the following guardian's home address or facility: _____

If Available Please Complete:
Parent/Guardian Name: _____
Contact Number: _____ Contact Email: _____

Supervising Agency: _____ Name of Pre-trial/Probation Officer: _____
Contact Number: _____ Contact Email: _____

Name of County Caseworker: _____ (if open case)
Contact Number: _____ Contact Email: _____
Other Contacts:
Other: _____ Contact number and/or email: _____
Other: _____ Contact number and/or email: _____

Additional information for school district:

Check box if:

☐ Youth went home without services

☐ Youth is a voluntary case and Link received written permission to send notification of involvement.

☐ Parent declined need for educational support (juvenile justice)

☐ Education Advocate assistance is recommended

Check box if:

☐ Link Assessment displayed a need for educational assistance

---

This notification serves as an opportunity to initiate school/agency collaboration in assisting this youth. Should you review records and find this youth is experiencing academic difficulty in any form, please contact the supervising agency. If an agency contact is not provided, you can contact _____

Please call immediately with any questions.
Sincerely,
_____ Title: _____ Contact Information: _____

Appendix 2

Sample Education Advocate Referral Form and Release

DATE: _____ REFERRING PERSON: _____ AGENCY: _____

PH: _____ FAX: _____ EMAIL: _____

MAIN REASON FOR REFERRAL (and/or desired outcome): _____

STUDENT INFORMATION

NAME: _____ AGE: _____ DOB: _____ SEX: _____

ADDRESS: _____

LIVING: ☐ HOME ☐ KINSHIP CARE ☐ FOSTER CARE

☐ RESIDENTIAL TREATMENT: _____

PARENT/LEGAL GUARDIAN: _____

PHONE: _____ CELL: _____

SCHOOL INFORMATION

☐ GENERAL EDUCATION ☐ SPECIAL EDUCATION (If checked, please attach all Special Ed documents available)
CHILD STAFFED THROUGH A COUNTY BOARD?
(Please attach report)   ☐ YES ☐ NO
IF NO DOES CHILD HAVE CONSISTENT ATTENDANCE?   ☐ YES ☐ NO

SCHOOL STATUS (past,present,future)	SCHOOL/FACILITY (city and state)	DISTRICT	ENROLL DATE	WITHDRAWAL DATE

(Attach a separate sheet for additional schools if necessary)

COURT INFORMATION

CURRENT CASES: _____ FUTURE COURT DATES: _____
LIST ADDITIONAL PROFESSIONAL/AGENCY WORKING
WITH YOUTH: _____
PH: _____ EMAIL: _____
ADDITIONAL PROFESSIONAL/AGENCY: _____
PH: _____ EMAIL: _____
ADDITIONAL INFORMATION PERTINENT TO THIS YOUTH: _____

_____

(Office Use) Date received: _____

Appendix 3

School Districts Student Enrollment Checklist

STUDENT NAME: _____ **DOB:** _____

If you intend to transfer a student from one school district to another, this is a list of community requested items that schools request upon enrollment usually along with a completed application.

- ❏ Up to date certificate of immunization
- ❏ Birth Certificate (passport or baptismal certificate may also be acceptable)
- ❏ Transcripts
- ❏ Attendance Records
- ❏ Discipline Records
- ❏ Proof of Residency (Ex: Deed, rental agreement, utility bill)
- ❏ Double check to make sure ALL forms are completed and signed.

If you do not have current transcripts, attendance and discipline on your child, please contact his/her last public high school attended before the Education Advocate to ensure those documents are secured.

YOUR SCHOOL ENROLLMENT MEETING IS: _____

AT _____

Appendix 4

Parent Interview

DATE: _____ PARENT: _____ STUDENT: _____

CHILD HISTORY

WHEN WAS THE LAST TIME YOUR CHILD DID WELL IN SCHOOL? _____
_____

WHEN DID HE/SHE START HAVING DIFFICULTIES? _____
_____

WEAKNESS/STRENGTHS AS A **STUDENT**? _____
_____

DO YOU KNOW GOOD WAYS TO HELP WITH SCHOOL WORK? _____
HOMEWORK ROUTINE? _____

PATTERNS OF BEHAVIOR/HOW DOES CHILD RESPOND TO STRESS? _____
_____

DO ANY APPLY?

    ☐SPED ED/LD _____ ☐EXPULSION _____ ☐TRUANCY DISTRICT _____
    ☐GIFTED/TALENTED

FEEDBACK

YOUR RELATIONSHIP WITH SCHOOL/IS THAT IMPORTANT TO YOU? _____

NEEDS TO BE SUCCESSFUL IN SCHOOL? _____
_____

WHAT SOCIAL SKILLS DOES HE/SHE NEED TO DEVELOP? _____

WHAT DOES CHILD NEED FROM AGENCIES : _____
_____

WHERE WOULD YOU LIKE YOUR CHILD TO ATTEND SCHOOL: _____
_____

NOTES: _____
_____
_____

Parent Contacts: _____
_____
_____
_____

Appendix 5

Sample Transition Summary

Student Name: _____ Birthdate: _____ Grade: _____

Current Facility name: _____ Placing Agency: _____

Date of initial placement: _____ Proposed date of discharge: _____

Name of contact person at facility: _____ Phone: _____

Name of Caseworker/Client Manager: _____ Phone: _____

Type of living arrangements:

         ☐ Home with Parents

         ☐ Home with Mom

         ☐ Home with Dad

         ☐ Living with Family Relative(s) other than parents

         ☐ Living with Family Friend

         ☐ Foster Home

         ☐ Group Home

         Other:_____

Name(s) of parent(s)/guardian(s) where student resides:_____ Phone:

                                                         H: _____

                                                         C: _____

Address where the child will be residing: _____

Current School District (if known): _____

Is student eligible for Medicaid?   ☐ Yes ☐ No

Will student be eligible for Medicaid once they return home? ☐ Yes ☐ No

Is this student on probation?   ☐ Yes ☐ No

If yes, name of probation officer: _____ Phone: _____

What are the specifics of adjudication?

Does this student have a mental health diagnosis?   ☐ Yes ☐ No

If yes, please list:

Is this student currently taking medications?   ☐ Yes ☐ No

If yes, please
list:
_____

Will this student be receiving any follow up services?   ☐ Yes ☐   No

Type of service: Contact Person: Phone/Email:
_____

Describe behavioral issues upon admission:

What were main treatment goals:
_____

Describe behavioral issues upon discharge:

What is the progress made towards treatment goals:
_____

Does this student have a SOMB specific containment plan?   ☐ Yes ☐   No
_____

Does this student have a behavior plan?   ☐ Yes ☐   No

Does this student have
a current IEP?   ☐   Yes ☐   No

                          Date of last Annual: _____Please include copy

                          Date of last Reeval: _____

What are his/her current academic levels:

Reading Grade Level:	As evidenced by:	Date:
Math Grade Level:	As evidenced by:	Date:
Writing Grade Level:	As evidenced by:	Date:
Full Scale IQ score:	As evidenced by:	Date:

Is youth prepared to deal with new academic setting? If not what does student
need to do to be prepared?

_____

**Are there any academic barriers that directly affect ability to learn in
a classroom?** (This would include trouble focusing, understanding instruction,
decreased problem solving skill, organizing materials, cause/effect, and/or feeling
unsafe in a classroom not otherwise related to a mental health diagnosis).

_____

What are his/her academic and personal strengths?

_____

What are his/her academic needs?

_____

What accommodations/modifications have been successful?

_____

What are the recommendations for level of services after transition based on the student's IEP and/or identified needs?

☐ Self contained classroom ☐ Day treatment ☐ Public school with support ☐ Resource room ☐ Other: _____

Is there any additional information that you can provide that would assist us in the planning for services or transportation for this student?

_____

Appendix 6

Education Intake Form: Court-Involved Youth

DATE: _____ NAME: _____ DOB: _____ AGE: _____ GRADE: _____ SCHOOL DISTRICT: _____

PARENT/GUARDIAN: _____ PHONE: _____ EMAIL: _____

GENERAL SCHOOL INFORMATION

CURRENT/MOST RECENT SCHOOL _____ SCHOOL CONTACT _____

CURRENT OR PREVIOUS OFFENSE ON SCHOOL GROUNDS: ☐ YES ☐ NO OFFENSE _____

SCHOOL STATUS: ☐ ENROLLED ☐ DROP OUT ☐ EXPELLED ☐ EXPULSION PENDING ☐ SUSPENDED

DATE OF EXPULSION (MONTH/YEAR) _____ REASON FOR EXPULSION _____

CHECK ALL THAT APPLY:
   ☐ SPECIAL EDUCATION ☐ LD ☐ ED ☐ SED   IEP CURRENT ☐ YES ☐ NO ☐ DAY TREAMENT _____
   ☐ 504 PLAN AND/OR BEHAVIOR PLAN
   ☐ CONTAINMENT PLAN
   ☐ GIFTED AND TALENTED   ☐ CURRENT   ☐ PREVIOUS   ☐ HOME SCHOOLING _____
   ☐ ESL PROGRAM   ☐ CURRENT   ☐ PREVIOUS

TOTAL HIGH SCHOOL CREDIT: ON TRACK TO GRADUATE ☐ YES ☐ NO
CREDIT RECOVERY NEEDED? ☐ YES ☐ NO ☐ UNSURE

CURRENT EXTRACURRICULAR ACTIVIES AND/OR SPORTS _____ HOBBIES/INTERESTS _____

☐ N/A GED PREP PROGRAM _____ STATUS _____ INTERESTED? _____

ADDITIONAL INFORMATION

HOW DO YOU LEARN BEST? ☐ WATCHING OTHERS   ☐ LISTENING TO OTHERS   ☐ WORKING WITH YOUR HANDS

DO YOU STRUGGLE WITH ANY OF THE FOLLOWING IN SCHOOL? (Check all that apply) ☐ None apply, I am doing well in school

☐ Regular attendance	☐ Staying in class	☐ Staying on task	☐ Leaving during lunch
☐ Conflict with adults	☐ Peer conflict	☐ Teacher respect	☐ Staying in school all day
☐ Fighting	☐ Behaviors in class	☐ Turning in homework	☐ Asking for teachers help
☐ Finishing school work	☐ Work is too hard	☐ Completing homework	☐ Peer pressure
☐ Motivation	☐ Classes too early	☐ Gang involvement	☐ Regular transportation
☐ Understanding material	Other _____		

DO ANY OF THESE STATEMENTS FIT YOU? (Check all that apply) ☐ No, I enjoy school

☐ I like school, I just do not like to do the work   ☐ I want to do well in school, but I am too far behind

☐ I do not like school and think it is a waste of time   ☐ I like learning but we never learn anything interesting

☐ I have too many other things to worry about and school is overwhelming

☐ School is not important to my family   ☐ School staff do not like me and do not want me there

☐ School is still important to me and I want to go back   ☐ I would like help in getting back into school or GED program

EDUCATIONAL INTAKE FORM:
COURT-INVOLVED YOUTH

BEST/WORST SUBJECT _____ DO YOU FEEL BEHIND IN ANY SUBJECT? _____

WORDS TO DESCRIBE YOU AS A STUDENT _____

ANY FEARS YOU HAVE ABOUT LEARNING _____

WHAT DO YOU HOPE TO ACHIEVE IN SCHOOL _____

TELL ME ABOUT WHAT YOU DISLIKE AND LIKE ABOUT SCHOOL _____

_____

WHO IS A SUPPORT FOR YOU? _____

ACADEMIC NEEDS

WHAT ARE YOUR HOPES AND DREAMS FOR YOURSELF WHEN YOU GROW UP?

DO YOU TRUST YOUR TEACHERS? WHO IS YOUR FAVORITE TEACHER? WHY?

DO YOU HAVE TROUBLE FOCUSING WHEN TEACHER IS TALKING? WHAT DO YOU FIND YOURSELF THINKING ABOUT?

DOES IT TAKE YOU EXTRA TIME TO COMPLETE SCHOOL WORK? DOES THE WORK HAVE TO BE PERFECT BEFORE YOU TURN IT IN?

ARE READING ASSIGNMENTS HARD FOR YOU? WHAT MAKES THEM HARD?

DO YOU HAVE TROUBLE MAKING FRIENDS IN SCHOOL OR SOLVING PROBLEMS WITH PEERS?

DO YOU FEEL SAFE IN SCHOOL? WHAT WOULD MAKE YOU FEEL SAFE?

DO YOU OFTEN LOSE TRACK OF WHAT IS GOING ON IN THE CLASSROOM AND STRUGGLE TO STAY ON TASK? (assignments, groups, discussions, read aloud)

DO YOU EVER FEEL ANXIOUS, FEARFUL, IRRITABLE, ANGRY, GUILTY OR SAD WHEN IN SCHOOL? WHAT DO YOU DO IF YOU HAVE THOSE FEELINGS IN SCHOOL? WHAT HELPS? WHAT MAKES IT WORSE?

TELL ME SOME GOOD QUALITIES ABOUT YOU! WHAT ARE YOU PROUD OF?

WHAT CAN WE DO TO SUPPORT YOU IN YOUR ACADEMIC GOALS?

FOR OFFICE USE ONLY: _____ Intake Only _____ School Notification _____ Home School with Services _____ Educational Services and/or Advocate Referral _____ Residential or Transition Program ©

Appendix 7

My Goals Worksheet

FOR: _____

DATE: _____ GOAL: _____

TASKS TO COMPLETE MY GOAL: COMPLETE

TASK 1 _____   ☐

TASK 2 _____   ☐

TASK 3 _____   ☐

TASK 4 _____   ☐

REVIEW DATE: _____ PROGRESS NOTES: _____
_____
_____
_____

REVIEW DATE: _____ PROGRESS NOTES: _____
_____
_____
_____

DATE: _____ GOAL: _____

TASKS TO COMPLETE MY GOAL: COMPLETE

TASK 1 _____   ☐

TASK 2 _____   ☐

TASK 3 _____   ☐

TASK 4 _____   ☐

REVIEW DATE: _____ PROGRESS NOTES: _____
_____
_____
_____

REVIEW DATE: _____ PROGRESS NOTES: _____
_____
_____
_____

Appendix 8

Sample Invitation Letter

September 3, 2018

Dear _____,

As an agency representative who plays a key role in helping improve educational outcomes for youth in XXXX County, I would like to invite you or one of your staff to collaborate on developing an Educational Action Team.

We share a common goal in our respective efforts to help ensure court-involved youth achieve greater educational success. As you know, studies show improved educational outcomes when there is more coordination between school and justice systems within the youth's community. The goal for the Educational Action Team is to work toward increased coordination and integration of care to improve outcomes for court-involved youth.

As such, we would be honored if you or one of your staff could join us as a representative of your agency and participate on the Action Team. We anticipate the time commitment will be minimal at first, as we are initially going to be gathering information on each member's agency protocols.

If interested, please contact us with the name and contact information for your agency's Educational Action Team representative no later than Month, Day, Year.

With your help, I am confident we can improve educational success for court-involved youth in XXX County. Feel free to contact me with any questions regarding this effort. I look forward to hearing from you, and thank you for your continued support.

Sincerely,

Agency Signature
Title

Appendix 9

Education Action Team
Meeting Agenda

Meeting Date: Meeting Time:

Meeting Attendees: Next Meeting Date:

Agenda Topics/Discussion:

Outstanding Actions:

Action Items	Status	Person Responsible	Due By

Action Items/Decisions Made:

Action Items	Status	Person Responsible	Due by

Appendix 10

Sample Action Plan

Mission:

Gaps in Service:

Strengths:

Identified Goals (YEAR):

Mission:				
Goal #1:				
Objectives	Plan of Action			
	Action Steps	Resources	Responsible Parties	Completion Date
Evaluation Criteria:				

Mission:				
Goal #2:				
Objectives	Plan of Action			
	Action Steps	Resources	Responsible Parties	Completion Date
Evaluation Criteria:				

Mission:				
Goal #3:				
Objectives	Plan of Action			
	Action Steps	Resources	Responsible Parties	Completion Date
Evaluation Criteria:				

Bibliography

Abbott, S. & Barnett, E. (2016). *The crossover youth practice model in brief: Improving educational outcomes for crossover youth.* Washington, DC: Center for Juvenile Justice Reform, Georgetown University McCourt School of Public Policy.

Allen, L., Almeida, C. & Steinberg, A. (2004). *From the prison track to the college track.* Boston, MA: Jobs for the Future.

Allensworth, E. M., & Easton, J.Q. (2007). *What matters for staying on-track and graduating in Chicago public high schools.* Chicago, IL: Consortium on Chicago School Research at the University of Chicago. http://consortium.uchicago.edu/publications/what-matters-staying-track-and-graduating-chicago-public-schools

Alvarado, R., & Kumpfer, K. (2000). *Strengthening America's families.* Juvenile Justice Journal, VII (3) 8–17.

American Bar Association & Casey Family Programs. (2008). *Blueprints for change: Educational success for youth in foster care.* Philadelphia, PA: American Bar Association & Casey Family Programs.

American Bar Association & Legal Center for Foster Care and Education. (2014). *Blueprint for change: Education success for children in foster care.* 2nd Ed. Retrieved from www.americanbar.org/content/dam/aba/publications/center_on_children_and_the_law/education/blueprint_second_edition_final.authcheckdam.pdf

American Youth Policy Forum & Council of State Governments Justice Center. (2018). *Leveraging the Every Student Succeeds Act to improve educational services in juvenile justice facilities.* New York, NY: Council of State Governments. Retrieved from http://www.aypf.org/wp-content/uploads/2018/01/Leveraging-ESSA-to-Improve-Outcomes-for-Youth-in-Juvenile-Justice-Facilities.pdf

Baglivio, M. T., Wolff, K. T., Piquero, A. R., Bilchik, S., Jackowski, K., Greenwald, M. A., & Epps, N. (2016). Maltreatment, child welfare, and recidivism in a sample of deep-end crossover youth. *Journal of Youth & Adolescence*, 45, 625–654. doi:10.1007/s10964-015-0407-9

Balfanz, R. (2007). *What your community can do to end its drop-out crisis: Learnings from research and practice.* Washington DC: Center for Social Organization of Schools John Hopkins University.

Blum, R. W. (2005). A case for school connectedness. *The Adolescent Learner,* 62 (7), 16–20. Retrieved from www.ascd.org/publications/educational-leadership/apr05/vol62/num07/A-Case-for-School-Connectedness.aspx

Brier, N. (1989). The relationship between learning disabilities and delinquency: A reappraisal. *Journal of Learning Disabilities*, 22, 546–553.

Brock, L., Burrell, J., & Tulipano, T. (2006). *NDTAC issue brief: Family involvement.* Washington, DC: National Technical Assistance Center for the Education of Neglected or Delinquent Children and Youth.

Brock, L., O'Cummings, M., & Milligan, D. (2008). *Transition toolkit 2.0: Meeting the educational needs of youth exposed to the juvenile justice system.* Washington, DC: National Technical Assistance Center for the Education of the Neglected or Delinquent Children and Youth.

Burke, A. (2015). Early identification of high school graduation outcomes in Oregon leadership network schools. Washington, DC: National Center for Education Evaluation and Regional Assistance. Retrieved from: http://ies.ed.gov/ncee/edlabs/regions/northwest/pdf/REL_2015079.pdf

Burke, A., & Nishioka, V. (2014). *Suspension and expulsion patterns in six Oregon school districts.* Washington, DC: U.S. Department of Education, Institute of Education Services, National Center for Education Evaluation and Regional Assistance, Regional Educational Laboratory Northwest. http://ies.ed.gov/ncee/edlabs

Casey Family Programs. (2004). *A roadmap for learning: Improving educational outcomes in foster care.* Seattle, WA: Casey Family Programs. Retrieved from https://humanrights.iowa.gov/sites/default/files/media/Casey%20-%20RoadmapForLearning1.pdf

Chien, N., Harbin, V., Goldhagen, S., Lippman, L., & Walker, K. E. (2012). *Encouraging the development of key life skills in elementary school-age children: A literature review and recommendations to the Tauck Family Foundation.* Child Trends Working Paper. Publication #2012-28.

Clemens, E.V. (2014). *Graduation and dropout rates for Colorado students in foster care: 5-year trend analysis (2007–08 to 2011–12).* Greeley, CO: University of Northern Colorado.

Clemens, E.V., & Sheesley, A. (2016). *Every transition counts. Educational stability of Colorado's students in foster care 2007–08 to 2013–14.* Greeley, CO: University of Northern Colorado.

Cole, S., Greenwald O'Brien, J., Geron Gadd, M., Ristuccia, J., Wallace, D., & Gregory, M. (2005). *Helping traumatized children learn: Supportive school environments for children traumatized by family violence.* Boston, MA: Massachusetts Advocates for Children.

Colombi, G., & Osher, D. (2015). *Advancing school discipline reform.* 1(2). Education Leaders Report. Alexandria, VA: National Association of State Boards of Education. Retrieved from http://www.air.org/sites/default/files/downloads/report/Advancing-School-Discipline-Reform-Sept-2015.pdf

Durlak, J.A., Weissberg, R.P., Dymnickl, A.B., Taylor, R.D., & Schellinger, K.B. (2011). The impact of enhancing students' social and emotional learning: A meta-analysis of school based universal interventions. *Child Development*, 82(1): 405–432.

Fabelo, T., Thompson, M., Plotkin, M., Carmichael, D., Marchbanks III., M.P., & Booth, E.A. (2011). *Breaking schools' rules: A statewide study of how school discipline relates to students' success and juvenile justice involvement.* Retrieved from http://knowledgecenter.csg.org/kc/system/files/Breaking_School_Rules.pdf

Farn, A., & Adams, J. (2016). *Education and interagency collaboration: A lifeline for justice-involved youth.* Washington, DC: Center for Juvenile Justice Reform, Georgetown University McCourt School of Public Policy. Retrieved from http://cjjr.georgetown/edu/wp-content/uploads/2016/08/Lifeline-for-Justice-Involved-Youth_August-2016.org

Farrington, C.A., Roderick, M., Allensworth, E., Nagaoka, J., Keyes, T.S., Johnson, D.W., & Beechum, N.O. (2012). *Teaching adolescents to become learners. The role of non-cognitive factors in shaping school performance: A critical literature review.* Chicago, IL: University of Chicago Consortium on Chicago School Research.

Finkelstein, M., Wamsley, M., & Miranda, D. (2002). *What keeps children in foster care from succeeding in school? Views from early adolescents and the adults in their lives.* New York, NY. Vera Institute of Justice.

Ford, J., Chapman, J., Hawke, J., & Albert, D. (2007). *Trauma among youth in the juvenile justice systems: Critical issues and new directions.* Delmar, NY: The National Center for Mental Health and Juvenile Justice. Retrieved from https://www.ncmhjj.com/wp-content/uploads/2013/07/2007_Trauma-Among-Youth-in-the-Juvenile-Justice-System.pdf

Fostering Success in Education: A National Factsheet on the Educational Outcomes of Children in Foster Care. (2014). Retrieved from www.fostercareandeducation.org/DesktopModules/Bring2mind/DMX/Download.aspx?EntryId=1279&Command=Core_Download&method=inline&PortalId=0&TabId=124

Gagnon, J. C., & Richards, C. (2008). *Making the right turn: A guide about improving transition outcomes of youth involved in the juvenile corrections system.* Washington, DC: National Collaborative on Workforce and Disability for Youth, Institute for Educational Leadership.

Gomperts, J. (2014). *Don't call them dropouts. Understanding the experiences of young people who leave high school before graduation.* Medford, MA: America's Promise Alliance Center for Promise at Tufts University. Retrieved from www.americaspromise.org/sites/default/files/d8/2016-10/FullReport%20DontQuit_23mar16_0.pdf

Gonsoulin, S., Darwin, M.J., & Read, N.W. (2012). *Providing individually tailored academic and behavioral support services for youth in the juvenile justice and child welfare systems.* Washington, DC: National Technical Assistance Center for the Education of Neglected or Delinquent Youth (NDTAC). Retrieved from www.neglected-delinquent.org/sites/default/files/docs/NDTAC_PracticeGuide_IndividualSrvcs.pdf

Gorski, Deb. (nd). What is response to intervention (RTI)? *RTI Action Network.* Retrieved from www.rtinetwork.org

Griller Clark, H., Mather, S.R., Brock, L., O'Cummings, M., & Milligan, D. (2016). *Transition toolkit 3.0: Meeting the educational needs of youth exposed to the juvenile justice system.* Washington, DC: National Technical Assistance Center for the Education of Neglected or Delinquent Children and Youth.

Gwynne, J., Pareja, A., Ehrlich, S., & Allensworth, E. (2012). *What matters for staying on track and graduating in Chicago public schools: A focus on English language learners.* Chicago, IL: The University of Chicago Consortium on Chicago School Research. Retrieved from https://consortium.uchicago.edu/sites/default/files/publications/ELL%20Report_0.pdf

Gwynne, J., Stitziel Pareja, A., Ehrlich, S., & Allensworth, E. (2012). *What matters for staying on track and graduating in Chicago public schools: A focus on English language learners.* Chicago, IL.: The University of Chicago Consortium on Chicago School Research.

Hendershott, J. (2013). *Reaching the wounded student.* New York, NY: Routledge Taylor & Francis Group.

Hoyle, J., & Collier, V. (2006). Urban CEO superintendents' alternative strategies in reducing school dropouts. *Education and Urban Society, 39,* 69–90. doi:10:1177/0013124506291983

Juvenile Law Center and Education Center. (2012). *Meeting the educational needs of students in the child welfare system.* Philadelphia, PA: Pennsylvania Developmental Disabilities Council. Retrieved from www.jlc.org/educatortools

KISR! Leadership Team. (2015). *Kids in school rule! Today and tomorrow. KISR!* Cincinnati, OH: ABA Center on Children and the Law, Legal Center for Foster Care and Education. Retrieved from: https://sc.ohio.gov/JCS/CFC/resources/local/KISR.pdf

Larson, K. A., & Turner, K. D. (2002). *Best practices for serving court-involved youth with learning, attention and behavioral disabilities.* Monograph series on education, disability, and juvenile justice. Washington, DC: American Institutes for Research.

Lewis, K.R. (2015, September 16). Why schools over-discipline children with disabilities. [Web log post]. Retrieved from https://blog.disabilityinfo.org/the-discipline-gap-how-children-with-disabilities-are-at-a-loss-in-the-classroom/

Lemon, J., & Watson, J.C. (2011). Early identification of potential high school dropouts: An investigation of the relationship among at-risk status, wellness, perceived stress, and mattering. *Journal of At Risk Issues,* 16 (2), 17–22.

Leone, P., & Weinberg, L. (2012). *Addressing the unmet needs of children and youth in the juvenile justice and child welfare systems.* Center for Juvenile Justice Reform. Retrieved from http://cjjr.georgetown.edu/wp-content/uploads/2015/03/EducationalNeedsofChildrenandYouth_May2010.pdf

Levy, M., Garstka, T., Lieberman, A., Thompson, B., Metzenthin, J., & Noble, J. (2014). The educational experience of youth in foster care. *Journal of At Risk Issues,* 18 (2), 11–16.

Louisiana Platform for Children Report. (2015). Baton Rouge, LA: Louisiana Partnership for Children and Families. Retrieved from www.louisianapartnership.org/Resources/Documents/Platform%20for%20Children%20Full%20Report.pdf

Macaluso, T. (2015, July 29). Sea change in student discipline. *Rochester City Newspaper.* Retrieved from www.rochestercitynewspaper.com/rochester/sea-change-in-student-discipline/Content?oid=2594965

Mac Iver, M., Balfanz, R., & Byrnes, V. (2009). *Advancing the "Colorado Graduates" agenda: Understanding the dropout problem and mobilizing to meet the graduation challenge* Baltimore, MD: John Hopkins University: The Center for Social Organization of Schools.

Maike, M., Nixon, A., Osborne, M., & Fox, T. (2016). *Washington's education advocate program: 2014–15 program evaluation.* Port Angeles, WA: Maike & Associates.

Morgan, E., Salomon, N., Plotkin, M., & Cohen, R. (2014). *The School discipline consensus report: Strategies from the field to keep students engaged in school and out of the juvenile justice system.* Retrieved from http://online.wsj.com/public/resources/documents/nydiscipline.pdf

National Center on Secondary Education and Transition. (2006, March). *Facts from NLTS2: School behavior and disciplinary experiences of youth with disabilities.* Retrieved from https://files.eric.ed.gov/fulltext/ED492093.pdf

National Juvenile Justice Network. (2016). *Improving educational opportunities for youth in the juvenile justice system.* Retrieved from http://njjn.org/uploads/digital-library/NJJN_Educational%20Re-entry-snapshot_Mar2016_FINAL.pdf

Neild, R., Balfanz, R., & Herzog, L. (2007). An early warning system. *Educational Leadership,* 65, 28–33.

Office of Juvenile Justice and Delinquency Prevention. (2014). *Meeting the educational needs of systems-involved youth*. Retrieved from: www.ojjdp.gov/programs/commitment120814.pdf

Osher, D., Banks Amos, L., & Gonsoulin, S. (2012). *Successfully transitioning youth who are delinquent between institutions and alternative and community schools*. Washington, DC: Center for Effective Collaboration and Practice, American Institutes for Research. Retrieved from www.neglected-delinquent.org/sites/default/files/docs/successfully_transitioning_youth.pdf

Osher, T., & Huff, B. (2008). *A family guide to getting involved with correctional education*. Washington, DC: National Technical Assistance Center for the Education of Neglected or Delinquent Children and Youth.

Philliber Research Associates. (2013). *Beyond content: Incorporating social and emotional learning into the strive framework. Volume 1: Social and emotional competencies and their relationship to academic achievement*. Accord, NY: Philliber Research Associates.

Phillips, R.S. (2011). Toward authentic student-centered practices: Voices of alternative school students. *Education and Urban Society*, 45, 688–699. doi:10.1177/0013124511424107

Posner, L. (nd). Big ideas: Dropout prevention strategies. Clemson, SC: National Dropout Prevention Center for Students with Disabilities. Retrieved from www.ndpc-sd.org/documents/Evidence_Based_Practices/ALAS_Model_Description.pdf

Rankin, V.E., & Gonsoulin, S. (2014). *Early learning is essential: Addressing the needs of young children potentially at risk for system involvement*. Washington, DC: National Technical Assistance Center for the Education of Neglected or Delinquent Children and Youth).

Rosenkranz, T., de la Torre, M., Stevens, W.D., & Allensworth, E.M. (2014). *Free to fail or on track to college: Why grades drop when students enter high school and what adults can do about it*. Chicago, IL: The University of Chicago Consortium on Chicago School Research.

Roy-Stevens, C. (2004, October). Overcoming barriers to school reentry. (Issue brief #3). Washington DC: Office of Juvenile Justice and Delinquency Prevention.

Rubin, D., O'Reilly, A., Zlotnik, S., Hendricks, T., Zorc, C., Matone, M., Noonan, K. (2013). *Improving education outcomes for children in child welfare*. Philadelphia, PA: The Policy Lab Center at The Children's Hospital of Philadelphia.

Seigle, E., Walsh, N, & Weber, J. (2014). *Core principles for reducing recidivism and improving other outcomes for youth in the juvenile justice system*. New York, NY: Council of State Governments Justice Center.

Skyles, A., Smithgall, C., & Howard, E. (2007). *School engagement and youth who run away from care. The need for cross-system collaboration*. Chicago, IL: Chapin Hall Center for Children at the University of Chicago.

Smithgall, C., Gladden, R., Howard, E., George, R., & Courtney, M. (2004). *Educational experiences of children in out of home care*. Chicago, IL: Chapin Hall Center for Children at the University of Chicago.

Snipes, J., Fancsall, C., & Stoker, G. (2012). *Student academic mindset interventions. A review of the current landscape*. IMPAQ International Stupski Foundation. Retrieved from www.impaqint.com/sites/default/files/project-reports/impaq%20student%20academic%20mindset%20interventions%20report%20august%202012.pdf

Snyder, H. (2004). An empirical portrait of the youth reentry population. *Youth Violence and Juvenile Justice,* 2 (1), 39–-55. DOI:10.1177/1541204003260046

Stephens, R. D., & Arnette, J. L. (2000). *From the courthouse to the schoolhouse: Making successful transitions* (OJJDP Juvenile Justice Bulletin, NCJ 178900). Washington, DC: US Department of Justice, Office of Justice Programs, Office of Juvenile Justice and Delinquency Prevention.

The Colorado Education Initiative. (2014). *Colorado framework for school behavioral health services: A guide to K-12 student behavioral health supports with a focus on prevention, early intervention, and intervention for students' social, emotional, and behavioral health needs.* Retrieved from www.coloradoedinitiative.org/schoolbehavioralhealth

The Council of State Governments Justice Center. (2017). *Realizing the full vision of school discipline reform: A framework for statewide change.* New York, NY: The Council of State Governments Justice Center.

The Council of State Governments Justice Center. (2013). *The second chance act: juvenile reentry.* New York, NY: The Council of State Governments Justice Center.

The National Technical Assistance Center for the Education of Neglected or Delinquent Children and Youth. (2011). *Improving educational outcomes for youth in the juvenile justice and child welfare systems through interagency communication and collaboration.* New York, NY: Council of State Governments.

The National Reentry Resource Center. (2014). *Measuring and using juvenile recidivism data to inform policy, practice, and resource allocation.* New York, NY: Council of State Governments. Retrieved from https://csgjusticecenter.org/youth/publications/measuring-juvenile-recidivism/

The PACER Center, Inc. (2000). *Reaching out to parents of youth with disabilities in the juvenile justice system.* Minneapolis, MN: PACER. Retrieved from: http://www.edjj.org/reaching.html

US Departments of Education and Justice. (2014). *Guiding principles for providing high quality education in juvenile justice secure care settings.* (Washington, DC). Retrieved from www2.ed.gov/policy/gen/guid/correctional-education/guiding-principles.pdf

US Government (2015). Every Student Succeeds Act of 2015, Pub. L. No. 114-95 § 114 Stat. 1177 (2015–2016).

Wall, P. (2015). *New York City task force recommends new ways to reduce school suspensions.* New York, NY: National Economic & Social Rights Initiative. Retrieved from www.nesri.org/news/2015/08/city-task-force-recommends-new-ways-to-reduce-school-suspensions

Wiig, J., Tuell, J., Heldman, J. (2013). *Guidebook for juvenile justice and child welfare system coordination and integration: A framework for improved outcomes.* (3rd Ed). Boston, MA: RFK Children's Action Corps. Retrieved from http://www.rfknrcjj.org/images/PDFs/Guidebook-for-JJ-and-CW-System-Coordination-and-Integration-Cover.pdf

Index

Made in the USA
Monee, IL
04 September 2024

65246728R00101